HD Radio Implementation

HD Radio Implementation
The Field Guide for
Facility Conversion

Thomas R. Ray, III CPBE

ELSEVIER

AMSTERDAM • BOSTON • HEIDELBERG • LONDON NEW YORK • OXFORD
PARIS • SAN DIEGO • SAN FRANCISCO • SINGAPORE • SYDNEY • TOKYO
Focal Press is an imprint of Elsevier

Acquisitions Editor: Angelina Ward
Publishing Services Manager: George Morrison
Project Manager: Mónica González de Mendoza
Assistant Editor: Kathryn Spencer
Design Direction: Joanne Blank
Cover Design: Gary Ragaglia
Cover Images © iStockphoto

Focal Press is an imprint of Elsevier
30 Corporate Drive, Suite 400, Burlington, MA 01803, USA
Linacre House, Jordan Hill, Oxford OX2 8DP, UK

 Recognizing the importance of preserving what has been written, Elsevier prints its books on acid-free
paper whenever possible.

Library of Congress Cataloging-in-Publication Data
Ray, Thomas, 1960–
   HD radio implementation : the field guide for facility conversion / Thomas Ray.
     p. cm.
   Includes bibliographical references and index.
   ISBN 978-0-240-81002-7 (casebound : alk. paper)
   1. Digital audio broadcasting–United States–Planning. 2. Radio stations–United States–Equipment and
supplies–Design and construction. 3. Radio–Transmitters and transmission. I. Title.
   TK6562.D54R39 2008
   621.384'15—dc22

                              2007052990

British Library Cataloguing-in-Publication Data
A catalogue record for this book is available from the British Library.

ISBN: 978-0-240-81002-7

> For information on all Focal Press publications
> visit our website at www.books.elsevier.com

Transferred to Digital Printing, 2011

Printed in the United States of America

Contents

Introduction

Congratulations! You are about to embark on an adventure in radio broadcasting that can be compared to the adventure Marconi, DeForest, and Armstrong took in the early days of our craft.

It is a time of change in our industry and one of the biggest changes of all is in-band on-channel (IBOC) digital broadcasting technology, otherwise known as the HD Radio system, possibly the biggest advancement in radio since the introduction of multiplex FM stereo in the 1960s. October 10, 2002 is a historic day in the United States, as the Federal Communications Commission (FCC) voted that day on the Report and Order that selected the HD Radio system as the digital transmission technology for terrestrial radio broadcasters. That decision was reaffirmed on March 22, 2007 with the FCC's adoption of the Second Report and Order that further established the guidelines and rules for IBOC digital transmissions, including the authorization of AM IBOC at night. These new regulations became effective on September 14, 2007. HD Radio brings a different perspective on the medium to listeners. It has the potential to open up new avenues of revenue for radio station owners, and it requires a different way of thinking about how we take our product and transmit it to the masses.

While we all know that a radio station is a complete system, many of us think of the various components of that system separately. We sometimes make changes to the studio, the studio-to-transmitter link, the audio processing, the transmitter, or the antenna, and treat them as entities completely separate from one another. They are. With HD Radio technology, however, we must now think of how all the parts of the transmission chain join together and interact as that complete system. Any one component in the system can affect the performance of the entire system. This book will give you ideas on how to make them all play together nicely.

The scope of this book will be how to put an HD Radio station together and make it work. We will touch on theory, but only to the extent that it will help you better understand how and why certain things need to be done. This book will tell you, for example, the requirements that your AM station's antenna system must meet in order for the HD Radio signal to pass unimpeded. It will not tell you how to make the antenna system do this, as that is beyond the scope of this book and, frankly, every station is different. It would be very difficult to describe each and every antenna system problem and how to solve it.

After reading this book you will better understand the generation of the HD Radio signal and the fact that there are actually several parts of this signal. You will learn about the care and feeding of the data reduced audio codec used to transport the HD Radio digital audio from source to listener, and you will be shown how to get the actual HD Radio signal through the transmitter and antenna, and what can affect both. You will also discover that things we have been able to get away with in analog radio simply will not work with the HD Radio system.

This book is written for not only the seasoned broadcast engineering professionals, but also for those engineers who have not yet ventured into the HD Radio arena. It is written to be understood by station owners, managers, and operations directors as well. In this way, as you evaluate your facility for HD Radio operation, there will be a resource available to answer the questions, "what do we need to do?", "why do we need to do this?" and "why do we need all of these things?"

This book is also written in the style in which I prefer to write: as if you and I are sitting around sharing either a coffee or a beer. You have asked what steps are needed to convert your station to HD Radio technology, and I am discussing it with you. We will even take a trip to the station so you can see for yourself what you need and how it all works. We will start at the studio end and work our way toward the transmitter site. At the transmitter site, we will actually install the HD Radio equipment and make it work. You should expect to come away with a lot of knowledge, and have greater confidence in your ability to convert your station to HD Radio operation with little trouble.

The adventure begins now. Congratulations! You are about to open a new chapter in the annals of broadcasting history.

Acknowledgments

This book would not have been possible without the following people:

My deceased father, who introduced me to a disk jockey named Dick Robinson at WDRC in Hartford, CT when I was either three or four years old. This sparked the radio bug in me.

My mother, who always told me I could be and do whatever I wanted and encouraged me to stick with things through good and bad. It also helped that she used to win things off of Joey Reynolds' show, and we would visit WDRC on a regular basis to pick up her prizes. And I should mention that it is because of me that she got her first gray hair. When I was two years old, I took a bobby pin that my grandmother had dropped and, seeing as it looked about right, stuck it into the nearest electrical outlet. Maybe that sparked (no pun intended) the electronics bug in me.

My wife Sue, son Tom IV, and daughter Sarah put up with me and understand that radio to me is more than a job. It's an adventure, with long hours and silly projects sitting around the house. And I being locked away in my room downstairs – writing or talking on my Ham rig, or experimenting. And did I mention them tripping over yet another HD Radio that a company has sent me for evaluation? How many times have I pulled the dashboard in Sue's car apart to install yet another radio she has to learn to use? I love you all. Do you still recognize me after months of pounding the keyboard?

Rick Buckley, President of Buckley Broadcasting; Bob Bruno, former VP/General Manager of WOR Radio in New York; and Joe Bilotta, COO of Buckley Broadcasting. These gentlemen allowed me to take WOR into the world of HD Radio on October 11, 2002, and have cheered me on the entire way. Without their confidence, I would not have gained the knowledge or experience with HD Radio, and this book would not be in your hands.

Russ Mundschenk, Jeff Detweiler, Scott Stull, Tom Walker, and Bob Struble at iBiquity Digital Corporation for giving me the information needed to learn what is necessary to make HD Radio work.

Brian Sczewczyk, Geoff Mendenhall, and Rich Redmond at Harris Corporation for assisting me with information gathering, and taking the time to listen to make their products better for the broadcasting populace.

Frank Foti at Telos/Omnia/Axia. Frank was always around to answer processing questions for me and provide me with screen shots as needed. I promise, Frank, that I'll make it to Cleveland next summer (because I was writing this book this summer of 2007) to ride your steam train!

Noelia Santelli, Executive Assistant at WOR Radio, for putting up with a constant stream of people coming into my office (and traipsing past her desk) to talk to me about HD Radio, for putting up with blasting audio from my office when I was evaluating yet another HD Radio, and for having to constantly listen to yet another version of "when I was writing my book this weekend …."

John Bisset of Broadcast Electronics and Gary Liebisch of Nautel for providing information and screen shots – and putting up with a bunch of inane questions ad nauseum.

Jeff Hugabonne of WTIC in Hartford, CT, and Chuck Dube of WFCR in Amherst, MA. Chuck provided pictures for the book and Jeff observations on HD installation and operation, and a good laugh or two when I needed it.

And let's not forget the great David Layer of the NAB. David, foolishly, volunteered to proofread this book, correct me where necessary, and beat me up when required. It is because of him that you can actually read and understand these words. And that I need a large box of band-aids (just kidding!).

And for those I either forgot or did not have space to list: your encouragement, guidance, and experiences we have shared have helped make all this possible. Thank you.

Thomas R. Ray III, CPBE
New York, NY
Ham call: W2TRR
November 18, 2007

An Introduction to HD Radio Technology

1

1.1 What is HD Radio?

HD Radio is the trademark for iBiquity Digital Corporation's in-band on-channel (IBOC) digital radio system. While there are differences between amplitude modulation (AM) and frequency modulation (FM) band HD Radio systems, an HD Radio signal can be generally described as a digitally modulated RF signal that is transmitted around, under and along side the present-day analog AM and FM signals. It should be noted that, strictly speaking, a hybrid HD Radio signal actually has two components – an analog modulated component (the legacy AM or FM signal) and the digitally modulated component referred to here. These digital signals are composed of multiple orthogonal frequency division multiplexed (OFDM) subcarriers, which are transmitted at a level to meet the specifications of the RF masks (AM and FM) as mandated in the United States by the Federal Communications Commission (FCC), and as specified in the digital radio broadcasting standard (NRSC-5-A) of the National Radio Systems Committee (NRSC). Since the OFDM subcarriers of the HD Radio signals are contained within these masks, and are therefore considered to be contained within the allotted channel for a given station without allocating any additional spectrum, it is considered to be an "in-band on-channel" system.

Eventually, when the penetration of HD Radio receivers in the marketplace is sufficiently high (over 85%, for example), the broadcast industry and the FCC will likely support the rollout of "all digital" IBOC which will allow the digital subcarriers to be moved into the area presently occupied by the analog signal, and the power level of the digital subcarriers could then be increased in an all-digital environment, improving coverage and robustness. Since the FCC has not yet authorized all-digital operation, this book will be concentrating on the hybrid mode of IBOC operation which is presently authorized and being transmitted by thousands of broadcasters, with more going on the air every day.

The audio in the HD Radio system is input in Audio Electronic Society-3 (AES-3) digital format. The digitized audio is put through an iBiquity Digital Corporation proprietary perceptual audio encoder called "HDC" which reduces the amount of bandwidth necessary to transmit the digitized signal. The output of the encoder is used as the information which is modulated onto the OFDM subcarriers.

To listen to the HD Radio signal, a new radio which can decode the HD Radio signal is required. When using a new HD Radio receiver, if the listener is tuned to an analog-only station, he or she will hear the normal analog signal. If the listener tunes to a station transmitting an HD Radio signal, the radio will first demodulate the analog signal. Once it has acquired the digital signal, the radio will then "blend" over to the digital audio, and the listener will be hearing the digital audio. If the radio should encounter a problem with the digital signal, it will immediately blend back to the analog signal. In this way, the listener will not lose the station and will hear audio (either analog or digital) continuously.

The FM HD Radio signal has more spectrum space available than does the AM HD Radio signal, as the FM channel has been allocated greater bandwidth. Therefore, the FM HD Radio signal can operate at a higher data rate than the AM HD Radio signal. This greater data rate can be subdivided to allow additional audio channels (or advanced data services – see below) to be transmitted on the same frequency. As an example, a station would transmit its main channel audio programming (which is broadcast in the analog signal) on their HD-1 primary channel. They could add a second, digital-only audio channel (call it "HD-2") and transmit a completely different program format on that channel. This is called "multicasting" and can only be done on the FM HD Radio system at present, though there is talk that it may be possible with the AM system, giving one high quality monophonic channel to the primary HD Radio channel and a lower quality monophonic channel to a secondary channel. The FM multicast channels can be stereo if this is what is desired by the station, and if enough bits-per-second are available to support stereo operation on these channels.

The FM HD Radio signal can also be split to add advanced data services, such as the transmission of stock market quotes to various data devices, or the ability of the station to transmit album cover art to a listener's radio. This adds a new dimension to the listener's experience, and/or increases station revenue if this data capacity is leased out.

There are companies presently working on a way for an HD Radio receiver to tie into a listener's cellular phone so that, if the listener liked the song he or she was listening to, he or she could press a virtual "buy now" button on his or her cell phone and order the song or album. Yet another innovation that is in its infancy is "iTunes tagging." With iTunes tagging, a listener has the ability to "tag" a song he or she has heard on his or her HD Radio. The HD Radio would have the ability to download this tagging information to the listener's iPod or computer, and the listener then would have the ability to purchase the song or download online at a later time.

Additionally, title and artist data, called program associated data (PAD) or alternatively, program service data (PSD), is transmitted in both the AM and FM HD Radio systems. Analog FM already has the ability to transmit this information via the radio data systems (RDS), which operates on a 57-kilohertz (kHz) subcarrier in the FM baseband. PAD will be a new experience for AM HD Radio listeners, as their radios have the ability to display title and artist information for the first time.

Table 1-1 A comparison of the audio specifications of analog AM and FM with AM HD and FM HD Radio.

Service	Audio mode	Frequency response	Stereo separation	Dynamic range	Audio quality
AM analog	Mono	50 Hz to 5 kHz	None	60 dB	AM analog
AM HD main	Stereo	20 Hz to 15 kHz	70 dB	72 dB	FM like
AM HD backup	Mono	20 Hz to 10 kHz	None	60 dB	AM mono
FM analog	Stereo	30 Hz to 15 kHz	65 dB	80 dB	FM analog
FM HD main	Stereo	20 Hz to 20 kHz	70 dB	96 dB	CD like
FM backup	Mono	20 Hz to 15 kHz	None	65 dB	FM mono

Source: AM & FM IBOC Systems and Equipment by Jeff Detweiler, iBiquity Digital Corporation. Published in the NAB Engineering Handbook 10th Edition.

The listener's experience for AM HD Radio can be quite startling. The first thing the listener will notice is that the "muffled" sound of traditional analog AM radio will no longer be present. When an AM HD Radio receiver blends from the analog audio to the digital audio, the frequency response opens up from the 3.5 to 4.5 kHz audio passband of a typical analog AM radio to a frequency response of 50 Hz to 15 kHz. The digital audio, in addition to being easier to listen to because of the greatly expanded frequency response, will also be in stereo, with a separation exceeding 70 dB. The audio will be in stereo within the primary digital coverage area of the AM station; it will blend to digital mono and then to analog mono as the listener moves farther away from the transmitter.

The next thing an AM HD Radio listener will notice is that the buzzing, whistling, humming, and audio fades of analog AM radio will no longer be there. The AM digital audio signal is very quiet. When a station has a silent spot in its audio, it is truly silent. If the listener is driving and passes under a bridge, the audio does not drop out to a burst of noise. The listener simply hears the digital audio. There are, however, limitations to this. If the bridge is too large it is possible that the AM signal will either become too weak or distorted, and the HD Radio will quickly blend to digital mono, then to analog mono, and the listener will hear some noise. It is also possible that the digital signal will be fully listenable while the vehicle is passing under the bridge and play out its audio buffer, then quickly blend to analog mono after the vehicle emerges from under the bridge. In this case, the listener will hear an analog signal briefly until the HD Radio blends back to digital audio. Overall, the listener will find AM HD Radio a much better experience.

The FM HD Radio listener will not notice as dramatic a difference going from analog to digital as will the AM HD Radio listener. The frequency response of the analog FM signal is 50 Hz to 15 kHz. The frequency response of the FM digital signal is 50 Hz to 20 kHz. In most instances, audio subtleties will take up the additional audio spectrum space and many listeners will not notice; some, especially us older folks, simply cannot hear up to 20 kHz.

The FM HD Radio digital audio does not use audio pre-emphasis as does the analog FM signal. Pre-emphasis is utilized to boost the high frequencies at the FM transmitter by 17 dB at 15 kHz using a 75-microsecond (µs) equalization curve. This is done to suppress the inherent noise present in the FM modulation process. This high frequency boost generally requires that clipping be used on the high frequencies on the transmit side to prevent overmodulation of the transmitter.

The receiver utilizes de-emphasis using the inverse of the 75 µs equalization curve, decreasing the high frequencies as received. Depending on design factors and the quality of the parts used in the de-emphasis network, the de-emphasis may not be as accurate as it should be. This can result in audio phase shifting, in duller or brighter high frequency response than contained in the source material, and other distortions of the audio signal.

As a result of the FM digital audio not using pre-emphasis, the listener will notice that the high frequencies are smoother sounding and do not have an "edge" to them. Additionally, since the audio processing is not clipping the high frequencies to prevent overmodulation due to the pre-emphasis used on the analog channel, the audio spectral content tends to be closer to what is input to the audio processor. Some industry professionals have commented that the lack of pre-emphasized audio gives the FM digital audio a sound that does not "sound like radio." This is not necessarily a bad thing.

What the FM HD Radio listener will notice in the mobile environment is a lack of multipath distortion or "picket fencing," though most listeners do not know this distortion is due to multipath fading. Most listeners will probably refer to it as that "hiss-hiss-hiss" or brief fading that occurs on FM. The FM digital signal is fairly immune to this phenomenon, and it makes for a much better listening experience.

Keep in mind that to keep the digital signal within the allotted channel space of an AM or FM station, the audio is transmitted in a data-reduced format. While not perfect, the HDC perceptual coding technology used in the iBiquity HD Radio system is optimized for low (under 100 kilobits per second or kbps) data rates. You may have heard that the HD Radio digital audio sounds like "computer audio." This is not the case, and in general, the listener will have a good experience with HD Radio.

The audio in the analog channel and the primary HD Radio digital channel must be both time and level synchronized so that there is not an abrupt change for the listener when the radio blends between analog and digital audio modes. It should also be known that, due to the digital conversion processing time which includes error correction, it is necessary to delay the analog audio on the AM HD Radio system by approximately 8.4 seconds, while in the FM HD Radio system the delay is approximately 8.7 seconds. I will discuss ideas to handle this delay for a station, which monitors an off-air signal, in Chapter 2.

It should also be known that, because the HDC codec provides an audio stream in a data reduced format, audio processing methods on the digital channels must be different than techniques used on the analog channel. You will need to add an audio processor specifically for the digital channel. This will be covered in Chapter 4.

1.2 The HD Radio signal for AM radio

The HD Radio signal, as generated by the iBiquity exciter, and as transmitted, consists of 81 OFDM subcarriers utilizing one of two modulation schemes. Most of the subcarriers reside in digital sidebands starting at ±4905.5 Hz from the channel center frequency, with the last subcarrier being located ±14716.6 Hz from the channel center frequency.

The first set of subcarriers is located within the audio passband of the analog signal and is transmitted in quadrature with the analog RF carrier using quadrature phase-shift keying (QPSK) modulation. QPSK works by phase modulating the digital subcarrier, similar to FM, but the subcarrier frequency does not change except its phase relationship. The data therefore is transmitted by changing the phase of the QPSK subcarrier.

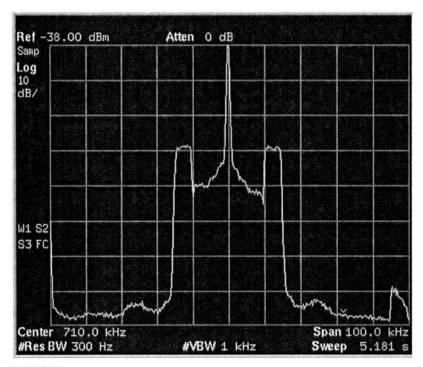

FIGURE 1-1

The AM HD Radio waveform.

The primary digital subcarriers carry the "core" audio. They are located ±10356.1 to 14716.6 Hz from the center of the channel, and are transmitted at a level of −28 dB as referenced to the unmodulated analog RF carrier. The secondary digital subcarriers are located ±5087.2 to 9447.7 Hz from channel center, and are transmitted at a level −43 dB as referenced to the unmodulated analog carrier. The secondary carriers carry enhanced audio data and are responsible for the stereo information contained in the digital audio signal. The tertiary digital subcarriers are transmitted from ±363.4 to 4723.8 Hz and are in quadrature with the analog RF carrier. The tertiary digital subcarriers are presently transmitted at a level of −45 dB referenced to the unmodulated RF carrier.

Finally, there is a "reference" subcarrier transmitted at ±181.7 Hz at a level −26 dB as referenced to the analog RF carrier, and two IDS subcarriers, transmitted at ±4905.5 and 9629.4 Hz, respectively, at a level −37 dB as referenced to the analog RF carrier. The IDS carriers contain information regarding a particular station's HD Radio operation which is used by the radio in the decoding process.

Table 1-2 The components of the AM HD Radio signal along with their placement and modulation types.

Sideband	Subcarrier number	Subcarrier frequencies (Hz from center carrier)	Frequency span	Power level (dBc)	Modulation type
Primary upper	57 to 81	10,356.1 to 14,716.6	4360.5	−30	64-QAM
Primary lower	−57 to −81	−10,356.1 to −14,716.6	4360.5	−30	64-QAM
Secondary upper	28 to 52	5087.2 to 9447.7	4360.5	−43 or −37	16-QAM
Secondary lower	−28 to −52	−5087.2 to −9447.7	4360.5	−43 or −37	16-QAM
Tertiary upper	2 to 26	−363.4 to −4723.8	4360.4	Data not available	QPSK
Tertiary lower	−2 to −26	−363.4 to −4723.8	4360.4	Data not available	QPSK
Reference upper	1	181.7	181.7	−26	BPSK
Reference lower	−1	−181.7	181.7	−26	BPSK
Upper IDS1	27	4905.5	181.7	−43 or −37	16-QAM
Upper IDS2	53	9629.4	181.7	−43 or −37	16-QAM
Lower IDS1	−27	−4905.5	181./	−43 or −37	16-QAM
Lower IDS2	−53	−9629.4	181.7	−43 or −37	16-QAM

Note: BPSK, binary phase shift keying.

Source: AM & FM IBOC Systems and Equipment by Jeff Detweiler, iBiqiuty Digital Corporation. Published in the NAB Engineering Handbook 10th Edition.

The AM HD Radio main channel has an audio bandwidth of 20 Hz to 15 kHz, a minimum stereo separation of 70 dB, and a dynamic range of 72 dB. Additionally, when all-digital AM HD Radio is someday authorized, two audio streams will actually be transmitted – "main" and "backup." The AM backup channel has an audio bandwidth of 20 Hz to 10 kHz, a dynamic range of 60 dB, and is mono. Audio quality of the AM main channel can be described as "FM like." Audio quality of the AM backup channel can be described as "AM mono."

There are two modes of operation for the hybrid AM HD Radio signal. The first mode, called 5 kHz mode, limits the analog audio bandwidth to approximately 5 kHz. The second, called 8 kHz mode, limits the analog audio bandwidth to approximately 9 kHz. No, that is not a misprint – the "8 kHz" mode name was originally assigned by iBiquity when the bandwidth was 8 kHz, and when the bandwidth was widened to 9 kHz the name was not changed.

In the 5 kHz mode, the radio constantly monitors the digital sidebands on either side of the analog AM signal and can choose to decode either one or both sideband groups, whichever will produce the best recovered data. I have participated in testing with the signal of WOR Radio in New York City which has shown that the digital sidebands of a hybrid AM HD Radio signal can be affected differently and independently by various causes. I have seen the lower digital sideband of the WOR signal literally disappear in the null of the antenna system on the northern portion of Route 17 in New Jersey. Even with the loss of the lower sideband, the digital audio was still being recovered properly, as the radio was getting its data from the upper sideband.

In the 8-kHz mode, the radio must constantly receive both of the digital sideband groups at all times to recover the HD Radio signal. In testing with the WOR signal, the coverage of the HD Radio digital signal was impacted significantly by operation in the 8-kHz mode, particularly in the null on the northern portion of Route 17 in New Jersey. Obviously, operating in the 5 kHz mode will make the AM HD Radio digital signal more robust.

Your station can also transmit PAD along with your audio. Depending on the software package and digital audio delivery system your station is running, you can put song title and artist on listeners' radios, put up messages based on time, and put up information associated with commercials. This will be a new experience for AM listeners and is something new for AM stations to bring to sponsors.

Additionally, the AM HD Radio system has "extra" data capacity that can be made available for sale, much like FM subcarriers. This data capacity can also be used for numerous purposes by the radio stations. AM HD Radio brings many things to the table that stations can use to their advantage.

1.2.1 FCC approval, interference, and nighttime operation

The iBiquity HD Radio IBOC system was granted an "interim authorization" by the FCC on October 10, 2002. As part of that authorization, AM radio stations were allowed to operate using the hybrid IBOC mode of operation

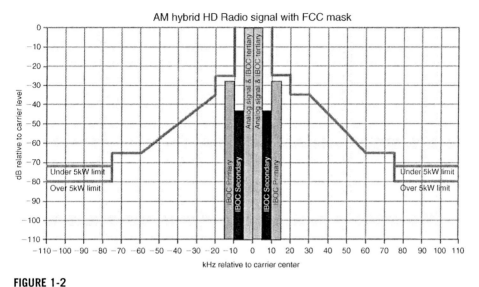

FIGURE 1-2

The AM HD Radio signal shown with the present-day NRSC mask limits.

from local sunrise or 6 AM, whichever is earlier, until local sunset or 6 PM, whichever is later.

Looking at the table in the previous section on HD Radio subcarrier placement in the transmitted spectrum, it is obvious that the energy of the HD Radio subcarriers is transmitted not only within the ±10 kHz used by the station's analog signal, but on the frequencies which may be occupied by first and second adjacent channel signals, as well. The energy of the primary and secondary HD Radio subcarriers which exists in these adjacent channel regions is well below the specification of the NRSC (and FCC) mask, as the system was designed to operate within the mask so that it would be compliant with FCC rules.

Due to its spectral occupancy, the AM hybrid HD Radio signal may cause unintended interference to first and second adjacent neighbors of a station transmitting an HD Radio signal. iBiquity has performed a great deal of analysis of AM radio stations throughout the United States, both analyzing the station's coverage as specified through antenna proofs of performance on file with the FCC, and through field strength measurements on both HD Radio and non-HD Radio stations.[1] This information has showed

---

[1] See, for example, "AM Nighttime Compatibility Study Report," iBiquity Digital Corporation, May 23, 2003.

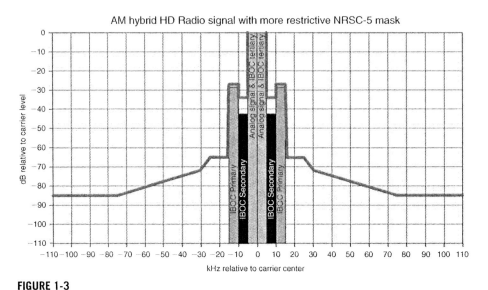

FIGURE 1-3

The NRSC-5-A mask. Note that the limits are much more stringent than the mask for analog AM specified in NRSC-2-A.

that only a handful of stations would likely experience interference within their normal nighttime interference-free coverage contours.

This is particularly important information, especially where it concerns nighttime operation of AM HD Radio. As the atmosphere cools starting at sunset, the ionosphere moves closer to the Earth's surface. When this happens, AM radio signals are reflected off of the ionosphere and can travel great distances, much farther than they do as a result of normal, "ground-wave" coverage. The resultant "skywave" signals have the potential to cause interference to co-channel and adjacent channel stations, hundreds, and in some cases, thousands of miles away. Consequently, one aspect of the iBiquity nighttime testing was designed to determine the effect of skywave propagation on co-channel and adjacent channel signals.

I participated in hybrid AM IBOC nighttime testing utilizing signals from stations WOR and WLW. WOR is on 710 kHz, located in New York City, with the transmitter located in Rutherford, New Jersey. WLW is located in Cincinnati, Ohio, with the transmitter located in Mason, Ohio, and operates on 700 kHz. Both stations operate with 50,000 watts. These tests were conducted over three nights in December 2002.

Both WOR and WLW were operating with a special version of the iBiquity operating software created specifically for this test. This software was synchronized at both stations by iBiquity engineers, and would turn on the

HD Radio subcarriers at WOR, and simultaneously turn them off at WLW. Several minutes later, the HD Radio subcarriers at WOR would turn off, and the HD Radio subcarriers at WLW would turn on.

The iBiquity test van used in the New York tests contained a spectrum analyzer, an iBiquity HD Radio test receiver, and a computer running specialized software that would record spectrum analyzer measurements, audio, and data on the HD Radio signal recovered from the test radio. The van also included a myriad of analog radios, including a home tuner, a General Electric SuperRadio III, and a few others whose names I forget. All were typical radios that could easily be found and available for use by consumers. The only modifications to these radios were to make the audio output signal directly available for recording purposes (if these radios did not already have that facility).

A listening location was chosen in Pennsylvania, in a parking lot alongside Interstate 78. The WOR signal, as measured with a calibrated Potomac Instruments FIM-41 field intensity meter was just about 0.5 millivolt per meter. The consumer radios were set up outside the vehicle, each connected to the recording computer.

When the WLW HD Radio subcarriers were on, a very slight hiss was heard under the WOR programming. When the WOR HD Radio subcarriers were on, WLW could still be heard, though there was a hiss under their signal. It should be noted that these evenings were very active skywave nights, and the level of noise under the WLW signal with the WOR HD Radio subcarriers off was the same as when they were on.

Another listening location was chosen in Allentown, Pennsylvania, again in a parking lot alongside Interstate 78. This was skywave territory, and we were outside the WOR 0.5 millivolt per meter contour. Again, the radios were placed outside the vehicle and connected to the recording computer.

Under skywave conditions, if the WOR HD Radio digital subcarriers were on and the WLW signal strength was equal to or exceeded the WOR signal strength, WLW was very easy to listen to. If the WOR signal strength increased beyond the level of the WLW signal, WLW would be unlistenable. It worked the same way for the WOR signal when the WLW HD Radio digital subcarriers were on. It must be noted, however, that when either station was severely interfered with by the other HD Radio digital subcarriers, if those subcarriers were turned off, the level of noise on the band was just as bad. My analysis of the situation was that there was very little interference being caused by the HD Radio digital subcarriers, and that the majority of the interference experienced during these tests was caused simply by skywave conditions.

Based on tests such as the aforementioned, the FCC approved use of HD Radio on AM stations during nighttime hours in their Second Report and Order issued March 22, 2007. This authorization took effect on September 14, 2007.

1.3 The HD Radio signal for FM radio

The FM hybrid HD Radio signal operating in the primary mode of MP1 consists of 190 OFDM subcarriers starting at ±129,361 Hz from the channel center frequency and ending at ±198,302 Hz from the channel center frequency. These OFDM subcarriers are the primary set of subcarriers for the FM hybrid HD Radio signal, and operate at a data rate of 98.4 kbps. The level of these subcarriers, compared to the unmodulated FM carrier, is −45.8 dBc. None of these subcarriers are contained within the analog audio passband as is the case with the AM HD Radio signal. It should be noted that these levels will allow the FM HD Radio waveform to fit within the FCC mask for FM stations.

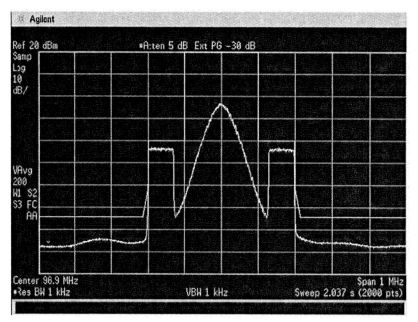

FIGURE 1-4

The FM HD Radio waveform.

It is important that the FM HD Radio subcarrier levels be compared to the unmodulated FM carrier for purposes of establishing compliance with the mask. Don't forget that when modulated, the FM carrier level will be constantly changing and in many cases the carrier will disappear, as the total energy of the sidebands cannot exceed total carrier power in FM. This is as opposed to AM modulation, where the sideband energy is added to the carrier and the (unmodulated) carrier level is constant.

An FM station has several choices available on how to utilize the available 98.4 kbps data capacity. One is to use the entire 98.4 kbps for the main channel audio. Because the FM HD Radio system has more bandwidth available and can operate at a faster data rate than the AM HD Radio system, it is possible to subdivide the available data capacity and add additional audio channels, called multicast channels. Contrary to what you may have heard, the digital coverage of a multicast channel will equal that of the main HD Radio digital audio channel – they are contained within the same data stream that is transmitted and do not operate at different power levels. However, the multicast channels will not blend to analog when the main channel audio does, but instead will mute. The station also has an available data capacity of 860 bits per second which can be utilized for many different purposes. Incorporation of PAD information and station information is standard as with the AM HD Radio system.

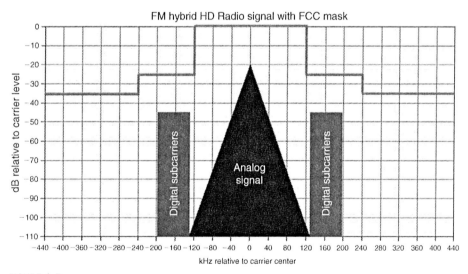

FIGURE 1-5

The FM Hybrid HD Radio waveform with the FCC mask.

A station could, for example, run the main digital audio channel at 64 kbps and add a second digital audio channel, which could be another program format, and run it at 32 kbps. At this data rate, the second digital channel would be stereo and have pretty much the same frequency response of the main digital audio channel, though the data reduction would be greater with a greater possibility of hearing data reduction artifacts.

The station could also subdivide the available 98.4 kbps into three different stereo audio channels to provide, say, two program formats, with the third digital channel being used for a radio reading service. There are many choices to make, which will be discussed in Chapters 4 and 6. It should be noted, however, that there is a point where reducing the data rate will affect the audio characteristics of the main digital audio channel. The FCC, in their Second Report and Order issued March 22, 2007, has stated that the audio quality of the main digital audio channel must be equivalent to the audio quality of the analog audio channel. This will vary by station, for example, a talk radio station will be able to achieve the required audio quality with a lower bit rate than will a classical music station.

If a station presently has 67 or 92 kHz analog subcarriers in operation, they are compatible with this mode of FM HD Radio operation, with one exception. 92 kHz analog subcarriers are not compatible with the extended hybrid mode of FM HD Radio operation (this is discussed more below).

The main HD Radio digital audio channel has a frequency response of 20 Hz to 20 kHz, with a minimum stereo separation of 70 dB, and a dynamic range of 96 dB. It can be described as "CD like." In the all-digital FM HD Radio configuration (not presently authorized by the FCC), there is a digital backup channel transmitted. It has a frequency response of 20 Hz to 15 kHz, a dynamic range of 65 dB, and is mono. For purposes of blending, this backup digital channel takes the place of the analog, that is, in the all-digital mode the main channel digital audio blends to the backup digital audio channel as impairments are encountered or signal strength at the receiver is diminished.

Since there is more room available in the FM channel, additional OFDM subcarriers, called Extended subcarriers, can be added to the FM HD Radio signal, and the mode then becomes the Extended Hybrid mode of operation. The extended subcarriers can be added in groups, called partitions. There are four available partitions that can be added in the extended hybrid mode. The maximum extra data capacity added by operating with extended partitions is 49.6 kbps.

A station operating with all four extended partitions will find them starting at $\pm 101,744$ Hz from the channel center frequency, and ending at $\pm 128,997$ Hz, at an operating level of -45.8 dB below the unmodulated analog carrier. Operating with extended partitions will adversely affect an analog subcarrier operating at 92 kHz. An analog subcarrier at 67 kHz and an RDS subcarrier at 57 kHz may notice a slight increase in signal-to-noise level, but otherwise should operate without problems.

An FM station operating in extended hybrid mode will have the ability to utilize the data capacity created by adding the extended partitions in a myriad of ways. It can be sold and utilized for data transmission by an outside company, providing an additional revenue stream for the station much in the same way analog subcarriers do. This capacity can potentially be utilized to provide album cover art to listeners' radios. There are uses for this data-casting ability that have not yet been dreamed up, but stations should know that it is available for their use. It should be noted that the extra data capacity gained from using extended partitions can also be used for the audio payload.

The actual transmitted power level of the FM HD Radio subcarriers, taken as a group, is 1 percent of the transmitted analog power. There has been much discussion regarding the possible need to raise this level. This is beyond the scope of this book, as testing is being done, but many hurdles would need to be overcome, including the re-configuration of existing HD Radio facilities to accommodate the additional digital output power.

There has also been much discussion regarding the possibility of interference being caused to first adjacent stations. As an example, a report was issued in 2003 regarding FM HD Radio that listed KWAV in Monterey, California, as a potential interferer to first adjacent stations on either side of their frequency of 96.9 MHz. This prediction was because KWAV is a "grandfathered superpower" Class-B station, operating at an effective radiated power (ERP) of 18 kW and a height above average terrain (HAAT) of 747 meters. Normal ERP for a Class-B station at this height would be 1.3 kW. The predicted 60 dBu contour is 49.46 miles from the transmitter.

The FCC, over the years, had allowed at least one first adjacent station to overlap contours with KWAV. It was predicted that this other station would lose a good portion of its coverage area if KWAV put on an HD Radio signal. KWAV did put on an HD Radio signal, and there have been no reports of interference to this first adjacent station.

HD Radio will be changing the landscape on the AM and FM bands for broadcasters and listeners alike. Now that we know what the HD Radio signal is, let's make it work, shall we?

The Studio Facility

2

2.1 Evaluating the studio for HD Radio operation

The studio facility is the point of entry for all audio into the transmission system of practically any radio station. This is where the programming is created and audio from various sources comes together to form the presentation to the public. There are many things to consider for the studio facility of an HD Radio station.

First and foremost, what condition is your present facility in? Contrary to what you may have been told, if your facility uses equipment of fairly recent vintage, you may be able to use it successfully in your HD Radio operation. If your facility is older, you are strongly urged to modernize your studio facility, as you will hear the difference on the HD Radio digital audio channel between your antiquated facility and your neighbor's new facility. Before we evaluate your studio facility, however, we need to understand a few basics regarding HD Radio.

An analog AM radio station's audio signal has an upper frequency response limit of 10 kHz. The analog portion of a hybrid AM HD Radio signal has an audio upper frequency response limit of 5 kHz (or 9 kHz, depending upon the mode of operation). The expected noise floor of the transmitted analog AM signal cannot be expected to be below −60 dB, and in fact will vary at a listener's location due to many reasons. The analog AM signal is monaural, though a station can choose to run a C-Quam AM Stereo signal. The audio for an analog AM stereo signal is limited to a frequency response of 50 Hz to 10 kHz. Stereo separation is rarely greater than 30 dB.

By contrast, the audio for an analog FM radio station has an upper frequency limit of 15 kHz, and is rolled off at this frequency to protect the stereo pilot. The expected noise floor of the transmitted analog FM signal is around −80 dB. The multiplex FM stereo system used in the United States utilizes a pre-emphasis curve of 75 microseconds, which causes a boost of +17 dB at 15 kHz. The analog FM audio can be stereo or monaural with

17

stereo separation rarely exceeding 65 dB. These analog figures need to be kept in mind when we look at the specifications of the HD Radio systems.

For an AM HD Radio digital audio signal, the upper frequency response limit for the audio is 15 kHz. The noise floor is in the area of −72 dB. The audio is stereo with a separation of 70 dB. For an FM HD Radio digital audio signal, the upper frequency response limit for the audio is 20 kHz. The noise floor is −96 dB. The audio is stereo and does not use pre-emphasis, and the stereo separation is 70 dB.

Table 2-1 A comparison of the audio performance characteristics of the AM and FM HD Radio systems to their analog counterparts.

Service	Audio mode	Frequency response	Stereo separation	Dynamic range	Audio quality
AM analog	Mono	50 Hz to 5 kHz	None	60 dB	AM analog
AM HD main	Stereo	20 Hz to 15 kHz	70 dB	72 dB	FM like
AM HD backup	Mono	20 Hz to 10 kHz	None	60 dB	AM mono
FM analog	Stereo	30 Hz to 15 kHz	65 dB	80 dB	FM analog
FM HD main	Stereo	20 Hz to 20 kHz	70 dB	96 dB	CD like
FM HD backup	Mono	20 Hz to 15 kHz	None	65 dB	FM mono

As you can see, there is a considerable difference in the audio performance characteristics of the analog and digital systems. Everything in your facility needs to be looked at, as there are things you can "get away with" in the analog world that you cannot get away with in the digital world.

It is extremely important to look at every aspect of the audio chain at your station. Paying attention to the details pays off in fantastic sounding HD Radio audio. Playing some of the "tricks" we do with an analog facility will become apparent on the digital signal, sometimes in surprising ways.

2.2 **The studio**

2.2.1 **Consoles**

Let's start with the audio console. What vintage is the console? If you are converting an AM station to HD Radio, the noise floor of the console must be greater than −72 dB while for an FM station, it must be greater than −96 dB. You will hear an elevated noise floor on the digital channel that you most likely have not heard on the analog channel. The cleaner the audio being fed to the digital channel, the better it will sound. If by chance you are still running a tube console, unless it is really clean with no filament hum and no scratchy step attenuators, it would be best to replace it.

Most consoles that have been manufactured since the 1990s should be usable for the HD Radio studio. These consoles generally use op-amps that are low noise, all the circuitry is direct coupled with no transformers, and the frequency response is almost "DC to light." They are also stereo by default, and since both AM and FM HD Radio signals can be stereo, this would be considered a plus. This does not mean that if you have an AM station and a majority or all of your source material is mono you need to immediately trash your source material in favor of stereo versions. The idea is to get your HD Radio signal on the air as clean as possible – stereo can come later.

FIGURE 2-1

When WOR, New York, initiated its HD Radio broadcasts, they were using 1978 vintage Pacific Recorders and Engineering consoles that were clean and acceptable for use with HD Radio technology.

At WOR in New York, we went on the air with our HD Radio signal using our original 1970's vintage Pacific Recorders and Engineering consoles which were mono. The PR&E Series One consoles were intended to be stereo, but WOR had serial numbers one through five, and the right channels had not been put into the consoles originally as they were "concept" consoles at the time. The consoles had very low noise floors, the frequency response was excellent, and the distortion was very low. Since we had previously replaced two consoles we had enough parts to put together the right channels in the remaining PR&E consoles and soon had stereo audio on the air. These consoles sounded extremely good, even though they were full of transformers. The transformers in these consoles were high-end Jensen transformers.

You will want to measure the noise floor of your console or consoles. The noise floor will need to beat the dynamic range of the HD Radio

FIGURE 2-2

When WOR, New York, moved their studio facility in 2005, the studios were designed as a digital facility.

digital audio signal you will be transmitting. You will also want to measure the stereo separation and frequency response. Stereo separation needs to be better than the specification for the HD Radio digital channel you will be transmitting. Typical modern audio consoles have a frequency response within a few tenths of a dB over the audio passband. You want the frequency response as flat as possible. If any of these measurements are out of spec for the HD Radio digital audio signal you will be running, or if your frequency response cannot be considered flat, you will need to consider replacing your console.

Additionally, you will want to measure the total harmonic distortion (THD) across the audio passband of the console. Typical modern consoles have a THD of less than 0.05 percent. You will then want to measure the inter-modulation distortion (IMD). The IMD of a typical modern console is also less than 0.05 percent. The less the distortion generated by your console, the better your HD Radio signal will sound on the air.

Before considering console replacement, however, you may wish to look a little closer at your console situation. Many times an elevated noise floor can be caused by such situations as a poor ground or ground loop, or simply by a noisy op-amp. You can check to see if there is a pin-for-pin replacement for the op-amps used in the console, as a newer replacement will most likely have a lower noise spec.

Noise issues can also be caused by sloppy wiring or loose connections, particularly on plug-in modules. Correcting a noise issue can be as simple as cleaning the contacts on card edge connectors by using a soft pencil eraser and rinsing both the circuit card edge and the socket with a good-quality contact cleaner. A prime culprit for noise can be the power supply. When were the power supply filter capacitors last replaced?

Frequency response issues can be caused by bad inter-stage electrolytic coupling capacitors, bad op-amps, or loose connections. Bad bypass capacitors can cause frequency response, separation, noise, and distortion issues. Power supply rails being out of tolerance can significantly raise noise and distortion levels.

If the console is solid state, of older design, and uses discrete transistor amplifiers, you may find that the amplifier design, coupled with input and output transformers, gives you significant IMD levels. If you really intend to keep your present console, it will need to be checked over thoroughly.

If you will be replacing your console with a digital console, you will need to look at the sampling rate of the system. The sampling rate can be thought of as the rate at which the system "takes snapshots" of the analog audio waveform. The sample rate used by the HD Radio system is 44.1 kHz, so this system is taking 44,100 snapshots of the audio waveform every second, for both the left and right audio channels (i.e., 88,200 snapshots total, per second, for stereo audio). While in general, using sample rates other than 44.1 kHz and then at some point converting to 44.1 kHz does not cause problems, if at all possible, you would want the other sample rate to be at least at 44.1 kHz or higher. I would also recommend that the console have the capability to perform sample rate conversion on the inputs if you will be connecting to equipment with digital outputs.

2.2.2 The microphone chain

Having a clean microphone chain is extremely important with HD Radio systems, particularly if you are a talk station or have a significant portion of talk on your station. Care should be taken with the components of the microphone chain.

First comes the microphone. It should be a good-quality microphone and be mounted in a shock mount. You may not hear certain things, such as people shuffling papers and putting coffee cups down on the counter-top, in an analog audio signal. You will hear this in an HD Radio digital audio signal. If the microphone in use has a roll-off switch, I usually leave it in the flat position. My preferred dynamic studio microphone is the Electro-Voice RE-27, which is hard to overload, takes a lot of abuse, has a good low end, and just a little brightness in the midrange.

If you will be using a condenser microphone, it also should be mounted in a shock mount as they are more sensitive to vibration noise than are dynamic microphones. Additionally, condenser microphones should be equipped with a good-quality pop filter. Condenser microphones are extremely sensitive to "popping" caused by quick sharp bursts of air resulting from the formation of certain consonant sounds. Equipping the microphone with a good pop filter will prevent that loud "thump" often heard when the announcer is too close to a condenser microphone.

You will also need to consider where the phantom power for the condenser microphone will come from. There are several possibilities: the console microphone pre-amplifier a pre-amplifier supplied by the microphone manufacturer, or from a microphone processor (if you use one). The phantom power source should first and foremost be of the correct voltage as specified by the microphone manufacturer, and it should be well-filtered to prevent hum in the microphone channel.

Finally, you may wish to consider putting a good quality attenuator on the output of the condenser microphone. Condenser microphones typically have a much higher output level than dynamic microphones, and it is easy to inadvertently overload the input of the microphone pre-amplifier. You will need to decide how much attenuation is actually needed. Too much attenuation will require the gain of the microphone pre-amplifier, to be increased, which will also increase the noise floor. Too little will cause clipping distortion on loud sounds.

It should go without saying that the microphone cable should be in good condition, along with the connectors used on the microphone, at the countertop (if used), and at the input to the microphone pre-amplifier. The microphone cable should be a good quality cable rated for microphone use. It should have an overall braided ground, be flexible, and be sturdy. You should try to avoid using "standard" shielded audio cable. Microphone levels, particularly for dynamic microphones, run around $-60\,$dBm. The typical console output is $+4\,$dBm. Computer monitors, AC power lines, fluorescent lights, and many other things found in a typical studio can cause noise to be introduced to the microphone signal. Using a good-quality microphone cable, and making sure the connectors are in good condition, is a good way to help keep the microphone signal clean. You may also need to consider the routing of the microphone cable, keeping it away from potential sources of interference.

FIGURE 2-3

The Wheatstone Vorsis microphone processor is an example of microphone processors found in broadcast studios. Note the amount of knobs and adjustments available. A little processing goes a long way on the HD Radio digital audio channels. Photo courtesy Wheatstone Corporation.

If your station uses microphone processing, you may find this needs to be readjusted to sound good on the HD Radio digital audio signal. Microphone processors should be adjusted with just enough compression to gently equalize levels among the various announcers who use the microphones. Do not use clipping in microphone processing (audio processing and the perceptual audio encoder are discussed in Chapter 4 – you will find out why there!). If you use equalization, remember that a little goes a long way. The most common mistake I see people make is setting the equalization controls at the extremes. A little equalization goes a long way in making the microphone brighter and punch through better. If you back down the compression, you will definitely need to use less equalization. When processing for HD Radio digital audio signals, less is better.

2.3 Source material

Of course, you have other audio sources coming into your studio besides microphones. Some, like CD players, or computer audio editors, you can do something about. Others, like satellite receivers, you are stuck with what the system is delivering to you.

It was mentioned before, and is mentioned again that the sampling rate of HD Radio audio is 44.1 kHz. It also must be kept in mind that the HD Radio digital audio channel is not a linear digital channel. It is a data-reduced channel, and if you can alter your sources to keep them at a 44.1-kHz sample rate and keep any digital audio in a non-data-reduced format, your station should sound extremely good over the HD Radio digital audio channel.

2.3.1 CD players

Compact disk (CD) players, as sources, are ideal. The sampling rate of a CD is 44.1 kHz. They are non-data-reduced linear sources. It is best to use CD players that have "professional level" outputs: XLR connectors at a level of +4 dBm. If you have a digital console with digital inputs, by all means utilize the AES-3 output of the CD player if it is so equipped. If your CD player uses consumer level audio outputs, it would be best to bring it up to pro level before putting it into the console. Make sure the matchbox you select will provide the noise floor to better the specifications of the HD Radio digital audio channel you will be transmitting.

2.3.2 Digital audio delivery systems

Digital audio delivery systems are manufactured by many companies, among them ENCO, Broadcast Electronics, and Scott Systems, to name a few. All of these systems perform basic needs for the broadcaster. They all record and play audio, and in some cases provide audio editing. How these systems handle the audio, however, varies greatly not only depending on the system itself, but on how the system is configured.

Many digital audio delivery systems utilize a central server to store the audio files. Most often, particularly on older systems, the audio files are data reduced to keep their sizes relatively small and maximize available disk space. These files are made smaller so that the computer network connecting the server to the workstations does not overrun, causing pauses or glitches on the air. This is also an economizing move due to the cost of hard disk drives.

There are also system requirements that affect the audio files based on the sound cards used. Many systems use a sampling rate of 32 kHz. Others

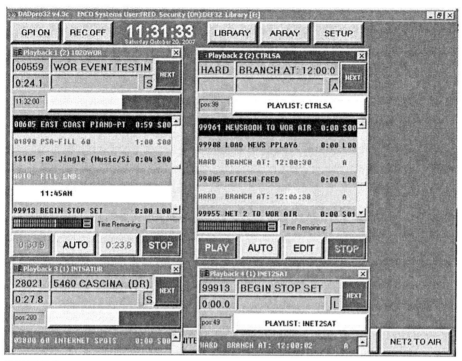

FIGURE 2-4

The ENCO digital audio delivery system, one of many digital audio systems found in broadcast stations.

allow you a large choice of the sampling rate to use. Unless there is a reason to run at a higher sampling rate than 44.1 kHz, such as needing to run at 48 kHz to properly feed a console input, I will run a digital audio delivery system at the HD Radio system sampling rate of 44.1 kHz.

If your system presently runs with a sampling rate of 32 kHz and you do not wish to change it, please keep this in mind. The upper frequency response limit is set by the sampling rate. The upper frequency limit is roughly half the sampling rate. A system sampling at a rate of 32 kHz has an upper frequency response limit of approximately 15 kHz. A system sampling at a rate of 44.1 kHz has an upper frequency response limit of approximately 20 kHz. The system using the sampling rate of 32 kHz would work fine on an AM HD Radio station, but the frequency response would be somewhat lacking for an FM HD Radio station.

Another sound card requirement would affect the audio quality. Most digital audio delivery systems encode the audio files in data-reduced formats, such as the MP3 standard. The data reduction coding, or data rate is specified in kbps, and a typical value is 192 kbps. This is different from the sampling rate, and will be explained more completely in Chapter 4. In a nutshell, the audio card samples the audio at 44.1 kHz, taking 44,100 "snapshots" per second of the audio. The encoder then goes through the "photo album" and throws out what it thinks your ear cannot hear. This runs at a specified data rate. The higher the data rate, the better the quality of the audio, as more of the original audio samples are still intact. On playback, the decoder takes the available audio data and recreates the audio waveform. The recovered audio, while being close to the original waveform, will not be exact because of the information that was discarded by the audio encoder.

Don't forget that the HD Radio digital audio signal is data reduced. The HD Radio system also uses an encoder that data reduces the incoming audio. If you are feeding linear audio data into the HD Radio encoder, it will be data reduced, and the resultant audio is only data reduced one time (since linear audio fed the encoder). If the incoming audio data has already been data reduced, the HD Radio encoder is going to reduce it again. The less data reduction used on the source audio, the better the resulting decoded HD Radio digital audio is going to sound. In any case, I would not recommend putting data-reduced audio through the HD Radio encoder that has been encoded (prior to input in the HD Radio system) at any less than 128 kbps. Anything less than that, and you will hear the artifacts in the HD Radio signal. They can be obnoxious.

Audio cleanliness is the foremost benefit for using a sampling rate of 44.1 kHz and linear digital audio. If your station is a music station, keeping the sample rate at 44.1 kHz and the format linear will also speed up your CD ripping operation when getting music into the system. This is because the computer does not need to convert the data copied from the CD to a data-reduced format.

If you intend to make changes to your digital audio delivery system, you need to consider whether your system allows audio segues on the same audio output. If it does, you need to be extremely careful not to mix sampling rates on a segue. This generally results in either a squeal when the segue occurs, which continues as the audio card cannot lock to the sampling rate of the new audio file, or the segue will be distorted, and the remainder of the new file will run off speed. It is generally acceptable to mix data rates on the same audio output. Check with the manufacturer of your system to be sure. You don't want any nasty surprises on the air.

The bottom line with your digital audio delivery system is that the audio should be as clean as possible. If you can run the system with linear audio data at 44.1 kHz, it will be superb. If you must run it with data-reduced files at a different sampling rate, you will need to experiment to find what combination of settings will sound best on your station.

2.3.3 **Digital editors**

Computer editing is another area of trouble in the studio. The audio card used in the computer should be a good quality professional card if you can put one into the computer. If you are using a digital console, it is best to use AES-3 inputs and outputs.

Editing programs, such as Adobe Audition, allow you to save audio files in many different formats. They also allow you to select the sampling rate, usually when recording to a new file. The sample rate should not be lower than 44.1 kHz. When you save a file, it is best to save it in linear mode, such as Windows PCM. If you must use data reduction, I find that AAC files sound much better when re-encoded by the HD Radio system than do MP3 files. In any case, make sure you select the highest data rate possible (for files that will eventually be re-encoded by the HD Radio system).

Saving audio in low data-rate MP3 format will have unintended consequences when used through the HD Radio system. Many advertising agencies send MP3 files coded at 56 or 64 kbps. These files, in general, sound perfectly fine through analog radio systems. Through an HD Radio digital channel, however, they have a peculiar "ringing" around the audio, almost like an audible halo. It is quite annoying. It is always best to use linear files into the HD Radio system, but if that is not possible, make sure to use or insist on data rates of at least 128 kbps.

2.3.4 **Satellite-delivered programming**

Programming via satellite delivery is common in most stations. The "dirty little secret", though, is that the audio delivered by the satellite receiver is generally data reduced. In the case of the Starguide system, a very common receiver found in stations, the data format is MP2. The data rate depends on the configuration the radio network is using and paying for.

While you cannot do anything about the audio being delivered to you via satellite, you must keep in mind the fact that it is data reduced if you record programming for later playback. We discussed earlier that the HD Radio encoder will data reduce any audio that is put into it, and using a linear file is ideal. We discussed your digital audio delivery system and that it should be run at a sampling rate of 44.1 kHz and linear if at all possible.

If you are recording satellite delivered programming for later playback, it is important that the audio in the digital audio delivery system be kept linear. The audio coming off the satellite receiver is data reduced. If you put it into a linear recorder, then play it back, it will be the same as if you plugged the satellite receiver directly into the HD Radio encoder, since the linear recorder does no data reduction.

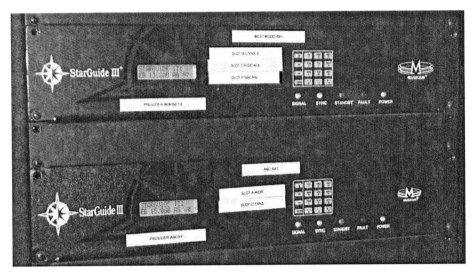

FIGURE 2-5

The Starguide satellite receiver. Chances are, your station uses one. Output audio is recovered from the MP2 format.

If your digital audio delivery system is using data-reduced files, the data-reduced audio from the satellite receiver is going to be data reduced when put into the system. On playback, this data-reduced audio will be further reduced, for the third time, by the HD Radio encoder. There are only so many times you can reduce the audio data before the data reduction becomes audible. This is called the "cascading effect" and has the potential to produce audible "artifacts" in the recovered HD Radio digital audio that will be unacceptable to your audience. The unacceptability of the artifacts depends on many factors, starting with the data reduction on the satellite end. This is why it is important to keep as much of your system as linear as possible.

The important point with the studio in an HD Radio facility is that the console be as clean as possible, and the source audio be kept as clean and as linear as possible. Data reduction can play strange tricks with your audio. Keeping it clean pays off in the end.

2.2.5 To convert or not to convert audio source material to stereo

Finally, you need to consider this if you are an AM facility about to convert to HD Radio technology: how much of your source material is in stereo? Some things you cannot do anything about, such as satellite feeds.

If your digital audio delivery system has all of its cuts recorded in mono, it is going to be a big job to re-record everything.

If your facility does not have much stereo material, that is OK and should not prevent you from turning on your HD Radio signal. Your listeners are already hearing you in mono. Turn on the HD Radio signal and let them hear a better quality, higher fidelity mono signal. Take your time and start adding stereo material the "right" way. You will not disappoint your audience.

2.4 **The studio environment**

I will keep repeating this theme throughout this book: you will hear things in the HD Radio digital audio signal that you have never heard on the analog signal. To give you an example, I have a friend who installed HD Radio technology on a classical FM/PBS station. At the time, HD Radio receivers were not yet widely available, and he had no way to really listen to this station in digital. We met at a regional convention and went out to my car, which had an HD Radio receiver installed, to listen to this station's digital audio.

The symphony that was being played sounded superb on the digital channel. The selection ended, there was the typical brief pause left by announcers of classical stations where there was absolute silence, then the microphone was opened and the announcer came on. There was a peculiar background noise under the announcer. My friend was upset.

We listened to the analog signal and did not hear this noise. We returned to the digital channel and listened for a while. I then asked my friend, "how many computers do you have in the studio?" It turns out that between computers and several satellite receivers, there was considerable fan noise in the studio. This fan noise was below the noise floor of the analog signal. But there it was in the background on the digital signal. My friend was flabbergasted!

I have also said before that attention to detail is important in putting HD Radio signals on the air. There are more details to be concerned with than just the audio handling. Go into the studio, sit in the announcer's position in front of the microphone, shut the monitor speakers off, and just listen. You may be surprised what you hear. Is there a ballast in a fluorescent light fixture humming or on the verge of humming? You will need to change it. You will hear it on the digital audio channel. Can you hear outside noises through windows? You may not be able to do anything about that, but you should look into what it will take to bring down the noise transmission through the windows. You will hear it on the digital audio channel.

FIGURE 2-6

Go into your studio – alone. Sit and listen to the environment in the room. You may hear noise that you have not heard on your analog audio channel, but you will, in all likelihood, hear it on the digital audio channel.

Look around while you listen. How many computers and/or items with internal fans are in your studio? You may need to consider putting the computers outside the studio and running keyboard/video/mouse extenders into the studios. You will hear the fan noise on the digital audio channel.

Grab the microphone and move it. Do the springs in the support arm creak? Do the joints squeak? You will need to consider either replacing the springs and lubricating the joints, or replacing the support arms. You will hear this in the digital audio channel if someone moves a microphone on-air.

Where is the air-conditioning vent in relation to the microphone? Can you hear the air moving out of this vent? You may need to move the vent to another location in the room, and add duct liner to the inside of the duct. You will hear this on the digital audio channel.

What condition are the studio chairs in? Go ahead – lean back and move around. Does the chair squeak? You may need to consider new chairs for the studio. You will hear this on the digital audio channel.

How about the door hinges? Open and close the studio door a few times. If the hinges squeak, you will need to lubricate them. You will hear this on the digital audio channel.

When we first put an HD Radio signal on WOR, we did not know what to expect. And no one on the morning show, which originated from Studio 2 in our old studio location, told Engineering that the door hinges squeaked. The first morning I had an HD Radio car receiver I kept hearing these noises in the background on the digital audio channel. When I arrived at the studio, I tried the door between the control room and the studio. The hinges squeaked. This was the sound I was hearing. I had never heard it on the analog signal, and the studio crew was used to the sound so never reported it. As I said, you will be surprised what you will hear on the digital audio channel.

You will need to thoroughly evaluate the environment in your studios that will feed the HD Radio signal. Another idea that may be helpful would be to put a digital recorder in the studio and walk out for 20 minutes or open the microphone in the studio and digitally record just the open microphone in the empty room for 20 minutes and then listen to the recording with a pair of headphones in a quiet location and really listen. You will pick up a lot of things you may not have heard before, and will need to decide if you need to do something about the sounds you are hearing. Don't forget – you will hear them on the digital audio channel.

2.5 Routers and audio distribution

Many facilities employ routing switchers and audio distribution amplifiers. Your audio routing will need to be evaluated as part of the process of converting to HD Radio operation.

If you are still using patchbays, there is nothing wrong with this method. It is simple, straightforward, and to the point. You should, however, evaluate the patchbays. If you have noisy jacks, you may want to consider replacing the noisy jacks or the entire patchbay. Look at your patch cords, too. Tarnished patch cord plugs will add noise to any connections you make with them. While it is difficult to find cleaners for these, I have had good luck with a product called Brasso. Put a little on a clean cloth, polish the plug with the product, and then rinse the plug with a good quality contact cleaner. The tarnish will be gone along with your noise problem.

If you are using other methods of routing, such as a routing switcher, you should look at the specifications and see if they are better than the specifications for the HD Radio system you will be using. Some routing switchers, particularly older ones, use banks of mechanical switches. You need to see if these are noisy and if so, they may need to be replaced.

We had one routing switcher at the old WOR facility that fed all channels to each room via big, fat unshielded ribbon cable. Unshielded. While the audio quality was acceptable, it was nice to see that system stay in the rack when we moved to our new facility.

If you have an older router, you may want to see if there are replacement op-amps available. Replacement op-amps can be much quieter and exhibit better audio bandwidth than their predecessors. You may also want to replace any electrolytic coupling capacitors in the router. And you will definitely want to replace the filter capacitors in the power supply to take care of any hum in the system.

If you are looking at putting in a new router, there are many ways to go and many companies to look at. You will have some decisions to make. Most routing systems offer a choice of analog or digital inputs and outputs. It is OK to mix and match – get what is right for your application. Make sure to find out what the internal sampling rate is. It should be at least 44.1 kHz, the sampling rate of HD Radio systems.

If you are putting in a new router, you may wish to consider adding router input and output nodes to your studios, rather than running audio cables from the studios to the rack room. This will make things cleaner from an audio perspective.

If you are replacing consoles and a new router is part of this process, you will want to see what the console manufacturer offers for audio routing. The console manufacturer's system will be built to talk to their consoles and both systems will "play nicely" together. This is important from the standpoint that you want to make sure you have no incompatibilities that will cause glitches in the audio. While the AES-3 standard defines many aspects of the digital audio interface, there are parts of it that are open to interpretation. Remember, the cleaner you can make your system, the better it will sound on the air.

2.6 Distribution amplifiers

I strongly advise against tying audio outputs together to feed multiple destinations. If you have two console inputs fed from, say, one satellite receiver, and one console has a problem on that particular input, it can affect the other console, possibly to the point of having no audio available. If you need to feed multiple destinations and are not using a router for this particular audio, you should use a good quality distribution amplifier.

A distribution amplifier takes the output from, say, your console, buffers it, and provides multiple outputs where each output of the amplifier is isolated from the other. In general, each output's level is also independently controlled from the others. Distribution amplifiers help prevent noise problems, grounding problems, audio level problems, and frequency response problems caused by excess capacitance from too much cable being tied across an output. While most inputs on modern equipment are in excess of 10,000 ohms, using a distribution amplifier will allow you to easily feed different impedance circuits without one affecting others. This makes for much more uniform treatment of the audio being distributed.

If you have the need to distribute AES-3 digital audio, you should *never* tie multiple feeds across one output. AES-3 audio outputs are intended to be matched to 110-ohm inputs. Tying AES-3 circuits together will cause an impedance mismatch which will distort the data waveform and cause glitches and audio loss from the data that cannot be recovered.

If you need to distribute AES-3 audio data, it is best to use an AES-3 distribution amplifier or passive AES-3 splitter. AES-3 distribution amplifiers are very similar to their audio-only counterparts, with the exception that most AES-3 distribution amplifiers do not allow level adjustment as there is no need to adjust the level of the digital signal, and the operating bandwidth is wider. AES-3 splitters present the proper impedance to the input and output signals to maintain data waveform integrity. Establishing proper data distribution to begin with will prevent unneeded headaches in the HD Radio facility.

2.7 **Analog-to-digital converters**

If you intend to keep your studio facility in the analog domain, you will at some point need to convert the analog audio to AES-3 data. This is done with an analog-to-digital (A-to-D) converter. The job of the A-to-D converter is to take your analog audio, sample it at the correct sample rate, and convert it to AES-3 audio. There are many A-to-D converters on the market. You will need to evaluate them and decide which one is best for your facility.

Most A-to-D converters will accept professional level audio at +4 dBm. There are a few models which have adjustable input levels. All A-to-D converters need to be told what the sample rate should be. Your A-to-D converter should be set to 44.1 kHz, the sample rate of the HD Radio system.

2.8 **AES clocking in the facility**

If you are running a digital facility, or a combination analog/digital facility, you need to synchronize the AES-3 clock from one source. Each piece of equipment has the option of running stand-alone on its own internal clock, or from an external clock source. Most have the option to use the external source and revert to the internal clock immediately should the external reference disappear for whatever reason.

The reason for clocking the entire facility from the same source is that the beginning of each AES-3 data frame is sent from each device at the same time, and that they are, and stay, in sync. Due to component tolerances, the internal clocking frequency of each device may differ slightly. With each device using its own internal clock, as time goes on, each device's data stream will be in a different position compared to other devices. This can lead to timing problems between devices, which can cause glitchy audio or, for example, a pop when switching studios.

It is best to choose an external AES clocking device, perhaps one node of your router or an A-to-D converter. Then, use an AES distribution amplifier to distribute clock to all your AES devices. Most routing systems have the ability to distribute the clock. If your system does this, you should take advantage of this utility to simplify matters. Using a master AES clock will greatly minimize many difficulties in your facility.

2.9 How to handle the HD Radio system delay

The hybrid HD Radio system requires that the analog channel be delayed by a certain amount: approximately 8.4 seconds for AM HD Radio systems and approximately 8.7 seconds for FM HD Radio systems. This delay is due to signal processing times of the digital audio and the transmission of error correction data.

The analog audio portion of the HD Radio signal is delayed at the transmitter with respect to the digital audio portion. When the HD Radio receiver first tunes to an HD Radio signal, it will produce the analog audio almost immediately. It will then acquire the digital portion of the HD Radio signal and, when the digital signal has locked, the radio will "blend", rapidly fading in the digital audio while rapidly fading out the analog audio. This blending will occur in the reverse direction (from digital to analog) if the digital portion of the HD Radio signal becomes impaired for any reason. Because the analog audio and the digital audio are time aligned in the receiver, the listener hears a smooth transition from analog to digital audio: usually only a change in the frequency response and overall quality of the audio. If the audio signals are not time aligned, the listener hears an abrupt "glitch" when the HD Radio audio blends, as both audio streams are in different positions in the audio. Because the analog audio heard at the receiver is delayed by approximately

8 seconds (with respect to a live transmission), this creates problems for broadcasters.

The first problem will occur at the studio. You will no longer be able to monitor directly off the air in your studios because of the HD Radio system time delay. This means several things.

How do you know if you are off the air? There are several ways this can be handled. If you have a transmitter control system that can either call out to the studio, or the engineer, or otherwise send up a red flag if the transmitter drops off the air, you can set up an alarm on this system. But this will only tell you if the transmitter is off the air. This will not tell you if, for whatever reason, there is no audio on the air.

Your best bet is to install a silence sensor with some type of alarm – either a strobe light or an obnoxious audio device – to get the attention of the person on the air to alert them to the problem. You should have an alarm on not only the analog signal (which is the signal that most persons are presently listening to), but also on the digital portion of your HD Radio signal and the multicast audio channels. You wouldn't want to be heavily promoting your multicast channel and find out it has been silent for several days because no one noticed. It is possible to have audio on your analog signal but have the digital portion of the HD Radio signal silent. There are two paths here. Things can and do go wrong with only one path. The audio processing and the HD Radio exciter are computers, after all, and computers sometimes need to be rebooted unexpectedly.

There are several ways to handle this. Several manufacturers make HD Radio monitoring equipment that can alert you to problems with your analog signal or any of your HD Radio streams. If you wish to do this yourself, there are several professional HD Radio receivers available, such as the Day Sequerra M2 or M4 or the Audemat-Aztec Goldeneagle HD Radio AM or FM, that will allow you to split the audio into analog on the left and digital on the right.

The next problem is: what do the air people listen to? The first thought that comes to mind is "program." If you have a talk station, the air staff most likely already listens to program because of the profanity delay, so they are already used to this. But if you have a music format, expect your air staff to be up in arms and start planning your demise when you make this suggestion.

This is because the typical air person is used to hearing himself and his voice mix over music with the air processing chain. He is not used to hearing the mix without compression, equalization, and limiting under him or her, and it becomes very difficult for them to judge audio levels.

How do you handle this? The best way is to take the old analog air chain and install it so that program is feeding the old air-chain equipment, and the old air-chain equipment is feeding either the headphone amplifier or the monitor position on the console. This will give your air staff the monitoring ability they need to be able to give their performance their all. You will also look like a hero. If you do not have an old air chain to install, you can either find used equipment to relatively inexpensively build an air chain, or go with equipment from one of several manufacturers that will give your air staff something comfortable to listen to. Another option being offered on some newer audio processors is to utilize the third output available to feed the headphone chain, as the audio is processed through the analog portion of the processor.

The HD Radio delay discussed above can cause problems with remotes. If you normally do remotes via phone line, either on telephone, or with ISDN or POTS codecs, you won't have a problem, as you are already feeding the location a mix minus. It must be clear, however, that if the location feeding on telephone has a monitor up for people to hear station audio fed from a radio, either the monitoring system at the remote location must be turned down or the talent needs to move away from it so that they are not confused with the resultant delay.

If you are doing remotes via remote pickup unit (RPU), this is trickier to handle. It is possible to ramp down the HD Radio delay for a remote. This function can be connected to the remote control, and the announcer on duty can hit the appropriate command to make this happen. This is, however, not recommended, as anyone listening on an HD Radio–equipped radio may end up with disjointed audio should his or her radio blend (between analog and digital audio) if the station is running an older version of the HD Radio exciter software. With a newer version of exciter software, the listener's HD Radio receiver will simply blend to analog audio when the ramp down command is given, and will not blend back to digital audio until the time delay is once again fully ramped in. The listener does have the option to force his radio to digital only mode during the time the delay is ramped out if his particular receiver supports this.

Probably the best bet would be to use a cellular phone for monitoring the feed from the studio. For an on-site public address system, the on-site talent's microphone could feed not only the RPU transmitter, but also a mixer. The cell phone could feed another channel on the mixer, and the on-site audio would be in real time while you maintain the HD Radio delay on the air. Another alternative would be to turn down the off-air feed of the station when the announcer cues the on-site talent via cell phone, then turn the off-air audio back on when the live shot is completed.

Another area of contention is live sporting events. Many times, fans will bring portable radios or televisions to the sporting event venue to watch replays or listen to play-by-play. Very often, the fans will receive information on, say, an injured player faster by listening to the radio than by waiting for any announcement made in the venue.

At the moment, the station can ramp down the HD Radio delay when the sporting event starts, ramping it back up after the game is over. As HD Radio receivers become more common, a point will be reached when the station will no longer be able to ramp out of delay. Each station will need to decide when this point will be. If the sporting venue seats, say, 30,000 persons, perhaps 1,000 of these persons will bring a radio to the venue. The station may well have 100,000 persons listening to a game. A decision must be made as to whether the station plays to the 1,000 persons who are sitting at the game listening to play-by-play, or the 100,000 persons listening who are being angered by not being able to listen to the game in digital because their radio will refuse to blend.

The real answer may be to install one or more Part 15 transmitters at the sporting venue for fans to listen to play-by-play in real time. In this way, the broadcast station does not need to risk angering the majority of listeners and can maintain the integrity of the HD Radio signal, while keeping the fans in the sporting venue happy by providing real time play-by-play.

While none of these suggestions will work for all stations, they are offered as a point of discussion. At some point, the station will need to address the issue of time delay and the need for real time audio in the field. Better to bounce this question around now rather than address it in a panic situation later.

The Studio to Transmitter Link

3

3.1 What is a studio to transmitter link?

Probably one of the most overlooked and neglected items in the path between the studio and transmitter is the studio to transmitter link (STL). The STL takes your programming from the studio location and delivers it to the transmitter site.

There are many different types of STL systems available. The most common types in use are:

- Telephone company dry pair, sometimes referred to as "twisted pair;"
- Telephone company equalized line;
- Telephone company T1 utilizing T1 equipment;
- Analog mono microwave (950-MHz band);
- Split stereo-analog microwave (950-MHz band);
- Composite analog-stereo microwave;
- Digital encoding over analog microwave (950-MHz band);
- Digital microwave (950-MHz band);
- Unlicensed Spread Spectrum (commonly the 5.8-GHz band); and
- Internet.

Each type has advantages and disadvantages. Some types are not recommended for HD Radio systems. Of course, if your studio and transmitter are co-located, you may not need to read this chapter.

3.1.1 Telephone company dry pair

While no longer common due primarily to the telephone company's switch to fiber optic cabling between central offices (COs), a dry pair (sometimes called a DC pair or copper twisted pair) is literally a pair of copper wires between your studio location and transmitter site. Typically, the pair was used on short-distance connections.

Many stations had used dry pairs for their remote control since, with no amplifiers in line, they were bidirectional. Being able to run DC on the line, stations could activate a relay at either end of the line to do things like shut down the transmitter if the DC went away (otherwise known as "the line is down"). Some stations have used dry pairs for their primary audio.

Being literally a pair of wires from point A to point B with nothing more than connection blocks in the path, the audio had the potential to be clean. Without a telephone-company amplifier in the path, and without the telephone-company equalizer at the receiving end, the station was free to equalize the characteristics of the line and amplify the audio as they saw fit. If two pairs were used and took the same path, they could be used as a stereo pair.

If your station is still using dry pairs, you will want to evaluate them to make sure they meet the noise floor specifications and frequency response specifications for the particular type of HD Radio signal you will be using. You may find that, while adequate for the analog channel, they may not work for the HD Radio digital channel.

3.1.2 **The telephone-company equalized line**

Many stations utilize equalized lines from the phone company. In an equalized line, the input audio is usually put through a transformer to change the impedance to 150 ohms, then sent to a phone-company CO. Lowering the impedance of the circuit allowed for greater audio bandwidth and less equalization than would otherwise be required, as the lower impedance would tend to lower the capacitance between the wires in the pair.

When the audio reached the first CO, it would go through a phone-company equalizer to flatten out the frequency response, then go through an amplifier, and the process would start over again until the end of the path was reached, where the audio would go through a final equalizer and amplifier to be delivered to the station.

The problem with these circuits is that the characteristics of the audio can be altered after passing through several transformers, equalizers, and amplifiers, and the noise floor is generally not as per HD Radio specifications.

In modern times, many phone companies use "digital equalized lines." These lines generally use data-reduced audio. The audio is input to the encoder at the studio, converted to a digital signal, and sent via data carrier between COs and out to the transmitter. At the transmitter, the data stream is converted back to audio.

If this is the method you use to get your audio to the transmitter, you will need to carefully evaluate the circuits for noise, distortion, frequency response, and, if stereo, audio phase shift. Since the audio is already data-reduced, I would think a station would want to avoid this type of circuit if at all possible, as the recovered audio at the transmitter site could produce artifacts in the resulting HD Radio digital audio. The HD Radio equipment will need to be at the transmitter site.

3.1.3 Telephone company T1

A T1 circuit from the phone company is a data circuit that runs at 1.544 Mbps. The phone company installs and maintains the data pathway between your studio and the transmitter site. What you do with the data pathway is determined by the equipment you plug into the T1. There are several companies that manufacture T1 equipment for broadcast use. One such device commonly found in radio stations is the Intraplex made by Harris.

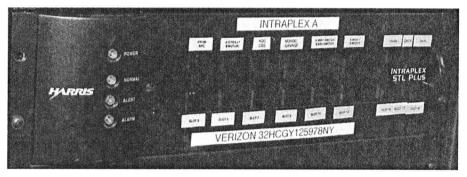

FIGURE 3-1

The Harris Intraplex STL/TSL system. This system, found in many broadcast facilities, typically utilizes a T1 circuit from the phone company. The system is bidirectional and can accommodate not only audio but also data, and other signals.

The T1 interface can normally be configured in many different ways. It will allow you to send non-data-reduced audio in either analog or AES-3 format to the transmitter site through the use of an analog or digital audio-encoder interface card. You can also add in Ethernet data capabilities to extend the station's local area network (LAN) which can be used with the FM HD Radio system to send the HD Radio digital audio data stream directly to the transmitter site. You can even extend the station's phone system to the transmitter over the T1, and run the data for the remote control system over the T1 which is bidirectional. If you want to place a satellite receiver at the transmitter site, you can receive your satellite audio over the T1 while you are sending programming to the transmitter.

If you need to utilize the telephone company to get your audio to the transmitter site, a T1 is really the best way to go. In most phone companies, the T1s are monitored and taken as priority if one goes down. They are reliable, and you have many options at your disposal. They are great for HD Radio STL use.

3.1.4 Analog mono microwave

Many stations are licensed to utilize a microwave path between their studios and transmitters in the 950-MHz band. Many AM stations use a mono analog STL. These are available commonly under the brand names of Moseley, Marti, and others.

In general, an analog mono microwave should be useable for HD Radio systems. It will need to be evaluated for frequency response, noise, and distortion to make sure it will meet the HD Radio standard for the particular type of HD Radio signal that will be used.

In general, however, if the microwave receiver has a good signal level, and the audio being fed is clean and modulating the STL transmitter properly, there should be no reason you could not continue using this STL until you are ready to go stereo, provided you put the HD Radio equipment at the transmitter site.

3.1.5 Split stereo analog microwave

Some stations utilize two mono microwave systems, with the radio frequencies separated by a few hundred kHz. These microwave systems are generally run together with one running the left channel audio and the other running the right channel audio. They work quite well.

If you have this type of microwave system, once again, you will need to evaluate it for frequency response, noise and distortion, as well as for stereo phase. If the system meets the HD Radio specifications, you should be able to continue using this STL system with your HD Radio installation, if your HD Radio equipment is at the transmitter site.

3.1.6 Composite stereo microwave

Many FM stations utilize microwave systems that allow the analog stereo generator to be placed at the studio, and the resultant composite stereo signal to be sent to the transmitter over the microwave path.

An AM station may be able to use this system if they have a method to demodulate the composite baseband audio at the transmitter site. Keep in mind, however, that you would be converting the audio to analog stereo baseband, then generating discrete left and right audio signals at the transmitter site. This can add noise and distortion and have frequency response problems, as the recovered audio will have gone through pre-emphasis and de-emphasis. You will need to fully evaluate the system to make sure it will meet the specifications of your HD Radio system.

Additionally, you will need to make sure that any audio processing you are using along with the stereo generator is minimal. Clipping the high frequencies too hard at the studio side will be audible in the HD Radio digital audio signal.

This system may also be useable for the analog FM audio on an FM HD Radio installation, though this is not recommended. It is possible to feed the analog exciter through this STL method, while delivering the HD Radio digital audio data stream to the transmitter site through another method, and delaying the analog channel audio through other means. I would not use it as a method to simply deliver the audio to the transmitter site for both the analog and digital signals, as the upper frequency response limit is only 15 kHz. Additionally, you will get artifacts in the HD Radio digital audio from the pre-emphasis/de-emphasis process. There is a lot involved using this method and whether or not to use it is entirely up to you.

3.1.7 Digital encoding over analog microwave

In the mid- to late 1980s, several manufacturers had digital STL systems that ran the data stream over an analog composite STL channel. One common system is made by Moseley and is called the DSP-6000.

The DSP-6000 system, in its day, was an extremely good alternative to the composite stereo analog microwave. The system allowed up to four channels of audio with a bandwidth of 15 kHz to go from the studio to the transmitter, and you would input the two primary channels in either analog or AES-3 format. You would take the primary channels out, either analog or AES-3.

The only problem with this system is that it is data reduced using APT-X data reduction. While it works well with an analog installation, you will most likely hear the data reduction artifacts on your HD Radio digital audio signal.

It would never hurt, however, to try this system. Just keep in mind that the audio bandwidth is limited to 15 kHz, and the upper limit for FM HD Radio digital audio is 20 kHz. Additionally, you would need a method to deliver the HD Radio digital audio data stream to the transmitter site unless you put the HD Radio equipment at the transmitter end.

3.1.8 Digital microwave

The latest series of 950 MHz band STL's utilizes digital modulation. One system is the Moseley Starlink. These systems allow you to transport

20-kHz bandwidth audio to the transmitter site in either analog or AES-3 formats. They also allow one-way Ethernet LAN connectivity, which can be used to transport the HD Radio digital audio data stream to the site for FM systems. Additionally, they also allow transport of RS-232 data which could be used for control purposes.

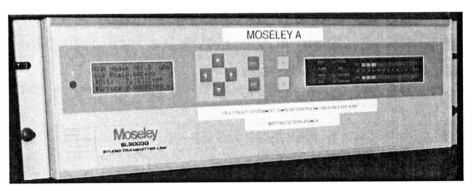

FIGURE 3-2

The Moseley Starlink receiver. Digital microwave systems are replacing analog microwave systems in broadcast facilities. The digital systems can accommodate more than one stereo audio channel and have the capability to carry unidirectional Ethernet signals.

If you are planning to use microwave for an STL, this is really the way to go. With FM HD Radio systems, it will allow the processor and HD Radio Exporter to be placed at the studio where the Exporter will be accessible in case a reboot is required. Digital microwave systems are highly reliable.

There are two things you should know about digital microwave. First, you cannot just install a system on an existing path. As silly as it sounds, you must go through frequency coordination to make the change to a digital STL.

I would highly recommend hiring a consultant to put together the paperwork and do the filing for the change. In the "good old days," the paperwork required by the FCC was minimal. The new forms are very confusing, and even if you know what you are doing, it is very easy to make mistakes and have your application rejected.

Second, the transmitter power-level is considerably less than your present analog microwave-system, typically 1 watt as opposed to the 10 watts or so your present system puts out. You will need to evaluate the microwave path, including the antennas, cables, and connectors, to make sure 1 watt will work once the signal gets to the transmitter site. It is not unusual to have digital microwave-systems running with a received signal level of −70 dBm or less. The typical system will run correctly down to around −89 dBm.

You may find that simply changing the antenna at one end of the path to a larger size will work out nicely. If needed, however, several companies manufacture amplifiers for the 950-MHz band that would boost the transmitter output to 10 watts. Typically, though, conversion to a digital microwave system is plug and play.

The digital microwave systems, however, are not without their quirks. The front end of the receivers tends to be fairly broadband. If your digital STL receiver is installed in an environment with 930-MHz paging transmitters nearby, you will need to install a bandpass filter for the broadcast auxiliary STL band in front of the receiver. In extremely hostile environments, you may need to install a channel pass filter in front of the receiver. WOR has an STL repeater installed at the 4 Times Square building. It required a channel-pass filter to be installed to reject the nearby 930-MHz paging transmitter signals.

Installing a channel pass filter will take care of other RF sources getting into your digital STL. It has an insertion loss penalty, though, on the receive signal level (for example, in the 4 Times Square installation just mentioned, this filter added 17 dB of attenuation). If your signal was marginal to begin with, you may need to change the antenna size, preferably on the transmit end, or you may need to install an RF pre-amplifier after the channel pass filter and before the receiver.

There are other tricks to make a digital STL system perform reliably. Among them is modifying the interlever coding to make the digital signal more robust. Consult the manual and the manufacturer of your system for more information.

The good news, though, is that the digital STLs perform very well in the presence of an adjacent channel or on-channel STL from another station. Both WOR and WBBR transmit on the same channel from Midtown Manhattan. The transmit paths are separated by approximately 80 degrees between their respective receive locations. While WBBR is using vertical polarization on the antenna, WOR is using horizontal polarization on the antenna. Neither station receives interference from the other.

3.1.9 Unlicensed spread spectrum

There are several systems available that operate in the unlicensed bands. At least two systems that I know operate in the 5.8-GHz range. Four "spread spectrum" systems that come to mind are the Harris Aurora, the Broadcast Electronics Big Pipe, the NXE-1 from Moseley, and the Axxcelera system from Moseley. These systems are bidirectional, and require the installation of antennas for the band in which they operate. One of the systems I know of operates with the actual transmitter indoors, while the others operate with the transmitter outdoors as part of the antenna.

Typically, these systems allow you to operate with the equivalent capacity of usually one or in some cases several T1 lines over the link. This would allow for the installation of a T1 system like an Intraplex to operate over the link. Additionally, some manufacturers have LAN kits available so that you could extend the station's LAN over the system. Some even allow you to send a phone circuit to the transmitter over the link.

The danger in using one of these systems is that, should interference crop up, the system is unlicensed. You would have no leg to stand on to get assistance from the FCC to mitigate the interference. If this were a critical system, for example, the *only* STL path to the transmitter, I would be wary. Some people report great success with these systems. I ran one at WOR for a while, then started receiving interference on the Times Square end of the link. Interestingly, several other stations were using these systems in the Times Square area and had no problems.

One other spread spectrum system operates in the 902- to 928-MHz band. It is the LanLink from Moseley. While this system utilizes unlicensed spread spectrum, it multiplexes onto the STL antenna and runs combined with your 950-MHz STL signal, so it uses an existing licensed path to the transmitter. Chances of interference are fairly low. This system provides you with Ethernet and RS-232 connectivity, and should be considered as an add-on to any 950-MHz STL system. Ethernet connectivity is almost a requirement at the transmitter site these days, and you will find out in Chapters 5 and 6 why it is required.

3.1.10 Internet

With changes happening at phone companies around the country, it is becoming more difficult to get some types of services, such as ISDN or T1, in many locations. Internet connectivity, however, is becoming commonplace. There are many companies offering audio transmission equipment using the Internet as the transport medium.

First, all of the Internet-based equipment I have seen uses data-reduced codecs. Most tend to use very high amounts of data reduction in an attempt to make the encoded signal that is sent via Internet smaller and more robust.

Second, I am personally still wary of the Internet as an audio transport medium. Broadcast audio is a "mission critical" service. Many things can affect the ability of the Internet to deliver the audio data packets in their entirety and in a timely manner from one end to the other. If there is, for example, congestion caused by, say, concert tickets going on sale, your station may find itself off the air briefly.

Due to the fact that Internet-based audio transport systems tend to use high amounts of data reduction and given the general nature of data transmission over the Internet, I would tend to shy away from an Internet-based solution. That's not to say this solution should be totally ruled out. If you are considering going the Internet route, proceed with caution and make sure you do all of your homework before making a commitment.

3.2 Remote control and subcarriers with digital microwave systems

3.2.1 Handling control data to the transmitter

Many stations send the data from their remote control system on a subcarrier – usually 110 or 152 kHz – on their radio STL system to the transmitter site. There is no way to accomplish this with a digital STL. There are no inputs for subcarriers.

The digital STL does have an available RS-232 port that is unidirectional, going towards the transmitter site. You will want to check with the manufacturer of your remote control system to purchase the modification kit for RS-232 operation on the side towards the transmitter. Most digital STLs have, as an option, a unidirectional Ethernet port that could also be utilized to send remote control data to the transmitter site. You will want to check with the manufacturer of your particular control system to see what they offer for options.

Conversely, you may wish to install one of the several available unlicensed spread-spectrum data systems which operate in the band of 902–928 MHz. One that comes to mind is the Moseley LanLink.

The data system typically installs between the STL transmitter and antenna at the studio, and between the STL receiver and antenna at the transmitter site, and contains a combiner to combine the two signals into one antenna on each end. Even though the data radio would be an unlicensed system, it utilizes an existing licensed path for your 950-MHz STL, so chances of interference are minimized.

The spread-spectrum data system usually has an Ethernet LAN connection and at least one if not two RS-232 connections available. It is a bidirectional system. You can easily extend the station's LAN and Internet access to the transmitter site in this way, in addition to having bidirectional data capabilities for the remote control. I have installed these at several stations, and they perform extremely well.

If you are using a T1 system through either the phone company or an on-air 5.8-GHz system, you are in good shape. The many manufacturers of T1 equipment have both RS-232 and Ethernet options, and a T1 is bidirectional. Check with the manufacturer of your remote control system regarding which way you will need to go.

3.2.2 **FM subcarriers**

Many FM stations utilize subcarriers, normally as a way to generate additional revenue. Very often, the subcarrier is generated at the studio and then sent to the transmitter over a composite STL. You will no longer be able to do this with a digital STL. If you intend to keep your FM subcarriers, you will need to deal with this issue.

You will need to move the subcarrier generators to the transmitter site and then need to get audio into the subcarrier generators, or data to the RDS encoder.

Most radio-digital STLs have the ability to carry additional audio channels. A microwave T1 system can also carry additional channels depending on how it is set up. You would need to put the subcarrier audio on an auxiliary audio channel on your STL and then feed this audio to the subcarrier generator at the transmitter site. Since most analog subcarriers do not have full audio bandwidth, the auxiliary channels on a digital STL can more than take care of their audio requirements.

3.3 **Summary**

In general, there are many different methods to use for your STL path. Most are at least similar to what you are probably doing now. You will need to consider the needs of the control system and getting audio to subcarrier generators. It is strongly recommended to use a digital STL, and have Ethernet connectivity at the transmitter.

If the STL system is selected wisely and is fed and set up properly, you can expect that your HD Radio signal will have a problem-free trip from studio to transmitter.

Audio Processing for HD Radio

4

4.1 What an audio codec is and how it works

In the previous chapters, we have stated that the digital audio on an HD Radio signal is data-reduced audio. Due to the constraints of the assigned channels on AM and FM stations, a non-data-reduced signal would be far too large to transmit. An audio codec is therefore used to remedy this situation.

An audio codec has two parts: an enCOder on the transmit side, and a DECoder on the receive side. These work in tandem to pass the audio from the transmitter through the RF channel and into the listener's receiver.

Unfortunately, I cannot give details about how the HDC codec used in the iBiquity Digital HD Radio system actually works. This information is proprietary and iBiquity would not release details for publication. I have been told, however, that the HDC codec has been optimized for data rates between 32 and 96 kbps. I will therefore submit a general overview of how codecs operate.

All perceptual audio codecs are based on a computer model of the human ear and on how humans *perceive* audio (hence the term "perceptual"; in the context of this discussion "perceptual audio codec" and "audio codec" are synonymous). The idea is to produce an algorithm that will, based upon our knowledge of human hearing, be able to remove parts of the audio that the ear normally would not "hear" under normal listening conditions.

To get this concept in mind, think for a moment about the human eye. It is easily tricked. At the movie theater, your eye will tell you that the characters are moving across the screen fluidly when in actuality, there are 24 still pictures being flashed on the screen in any given second. The pictures are changed so rapidly that the eye cannot perceive that they are individual pictures. The eye perceives the scene as having movement. It is the same idea with analog television, where an electron beam scans across the face of a cathode ray tube, drawing 30 pictures per second. Your eye

49

does not pick up on the scan lines or the changing pictures, but registers all the above as smooth motion.

The human ear can be tricked, as well. One example of this is the Arbitron portable people meter (PPM) system. It operates under the theory that the ear cannot hear one tone if it is placed next to another tone at a much higher level. The PPM system analyzes the incoming audio, then places its data into the audio in a series of brief tones, right next to and at a lower level than the normal audio. Your ear does not have the ability to pick out these bursts of data, and the listener is blissfully ignorant of the fact that the PPM data is being added to the audio.

The algorithm created for a given codec analyzes the incoming audio; determines, based on its knowledge of human hearing, what sounds the ear will not be able to notice are missing; and removes these sounds. In the case of HD Radio audio coding, the incoming audio is linear and sampled at 44,100 times per second. The data rate of the incoming AES-3 signal is:

44,100 samples/second × 16 bits/sample × 2 audio channels

making the data rate 1,411,200 bits per second (bps).

The HD Radio codec output data rate for the AM HD Radio system is 32,000 bps (alternatively expressed as 32 kbps). The codec is a busy beaver as it has to reduce this data stream by a ratio of 44:1. That's a lot of data to remove! On the FM HD Radio system, if your primary FM HD Radio digital-audio channel is running at 96 kbps, the reduction ratio is 15:1. At 64 kbps, it is 22:1. This is important to keep in mind as we go further into processing, and you will understand why I have stated previously that there are things a station can get away with in the analog domain that simply will not work in the HD Radio digital audio domain.

This is why I have also stated previously that your source audio, as delivered to the HDC codec, should be as clean as possible. Dirty audio can translate to really bad audio in the HD Radio digital audio domain, as the codec may remove good sounds and leave the bad ones in. As Cris Alexander, Director of Engineering of Crawford Broadcasting was so eloquently quoted in an article in Radio World Magazine, "You can make AM HD-R sound truly FM-like with good attention to details: proper load symmetry/orientation, low-compression/high data rate source material, high-bandwidth/low-compression or linear STL and careful processing. You can otherwise, with very little effort, make it sound really bad."

The codec will work on the audio and remove what it knows the ear cannot hear. It will then package this data, along with instructions for the decoder side of the codec, and ship it off for transmission. The instructions tell the decoder how to reconstruct the audio waveform, and also includes information so that the decoder can reconstruct data that may be missing in the form of lost packets.

In the radio, the HD Radio signal is demodulated, and the codec is presented with the data packets from the encoder side. The decoder must take the data it has been presented, look at the instructions, and reconstruct the original audio waveform as best as possible. If done properly, the human ear will not be able to tell the difference between the reconstruction and the original. If, however, there are data packets missing, or the source audio was bad to begin with, the listener will hear coding artifacts. If data packets are missing, the codec will look at the data presented before the lost packet(s) and the data presented after the lost packet(s), and reconstruct the missing data depending on its interpretation of what is missing.

In Chapters 3 and 4, I have discussed why it is important that your source audio be linear or, if it must be data reduced, to use the least amount of data reduction possible. Let us first consider the linear source. We will discuss putting the audio through the AM HDC codec.

The linear source will be presenting a data rate of 1,411,200 bps to the encoder. The encoder, in turn, is reducing this to 32,000 bps for the AM HD Radio system. Since it is the original audio that is being reduced, it will sound extremely good (as good as it can, using this codec) at the output of the decoder.

Now let us take a look at a data-reduced source. Your automation system has been presented with a linear source of 1,411,200 bps. If you are reducing it to 192,000 bps, you are reducing it by a ratio of 7.5:1. This audio will sound quite good.

Now you will take this data-reduced signal and put it through the AM HDC codec. You are putting a signal with 192,000 bps in, and in the case of the AM HDC codec, getting 32,000 bps out. Initially, you will think that the HDC codec is getting off easy, and technically it is. Reducing a 192 kbps signal is a far cry from reducing a 1411.2 kbps signal. But consider that you have already thrown out an awful lot of data from the original signal. The waveform as presented to the HDC codec is already missing parts. The HDC codec will now further reduce what it has been presented with. It may make some errors in its interpretation, because the information it is working with already has missing parts. This will likely cause audible artifacts in the output of the codec in the listener's radio. In many cases, the artifacts are not bad, and the average listener will not hear them. In some cases, however, the artifacts are extremely audible.

On remotes, we tend to run the ISDN codecs at WOR with the AAC audio-coding algorithm. We had been using MP3. We found that, with the MP3 algorithm running at the maximum ISDN rate of 64 kbps, the audio on the HD Radio channel had a peculiar "ringing" to it, almost like an audible halo. You will need to experiment to find what works best for your station.

My best guess is that the HDC codec being used by iBiquity in the HD Radio system is somewhat similar to AAC. I make this statement because I find that, if I must use data-reduced audio files, AAC coded files sound best going through the HDC codec. If you experiment with various audio codecs, you will find that further data reduction within the same type of codec will present fewer artifacts than if you have switched codec types. Experimenting off-line with digital editors, I find that I can come very close to the sound of the HDC codec if I use the AAC algorithm.

If you are not familiar with codecs and how they work, I would suggest that you sit down with an audio editing program and experiment. Record an audio source in linear mode; convert it to a data-reduced format, like MP3 or AAC; and see what it sounds like at various data rates. Take one of your conversions and save it. Open it again with the editor, and save it at a lower data rate and/or as another type of codec at a lower data rate. Compare the data-reduced files with the original audio and hear what happens. You will soon discover and begin to understand what happens as you cascade algorithms and data rates. It is a good method to understand how to feed the HDC codec.

4.2 Processing the analog and digital audio separately

As part of the process of installing the HD Radio system at your station, you will need to do the audio processing of the HD Radio digital audio separately from that of the analog audio. For AM HD Radio systems, one obvious reason for this is the frequency response difference.

The digital audio portion of the AM HD Radio signal has an upper frequency response limit of 15 kHz. The AM analog signal prior to the installation of the HD Radio system had an upper frequency response limit of 10 kHz (in accordance with the NRSC-1 standard). With the HD Radio signal, this will be reduced to 5 kHz, unless you choose to use the 8 kHz option for AM HD Radio transmission.

On the analog processor, you first need to roll off the high frequency response at 5 kHz. You then need to make equalization adjustments that will add some life to your 5 kHz frequency limited audio. If you do not tweak the equalization, the signal will sound very dull and muddy.

You will most likely be running a decent amount of compression on the analog audio, and will be hard clipping the output, in addition to running asymmetrical audio with positive peaks exceeding 100 percent modulation. Incidentally, regardless of what you may have heard, you may run up to 97 percent negative peaks and up to 125 percent positive peaks on the analog signal when you turn on your HD Radio signal.

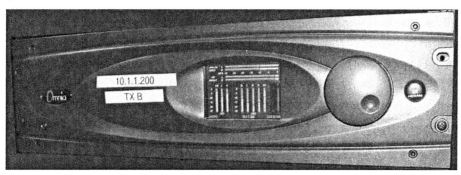

FIGURE 4-1

The Omnia 5-EX AM audio processor. This processor has outputs for both the analog audio channel and the digital audio channel. It allows completely different settings for both the analog and digital sides.

On the HD Radio digital audio side, you will have an upper frequency response limit of 15 kHz – considerably higher than the upper response limit on the analog side. The digital audio will be stereo, as opposed to mono on the analog side. The equalization points are purposely different on the digital audio side for better performance through the HDC codec. And you will not use hard clipping at all on the digital audio side. Most audio processors used on the digital audio side use various "look ahead" methods to pull down the peaks so that they do not become an overmodulation issue rather than hard clipping them.

When you hard clip an audio peak, two things happen. First, the top of the waveform gets clipped off, and in most cases, this prevents overmodulation and can also make the signal louder. Clipping, however, introduces distortion to the waveform and will generate harmonics that did not exist in the original audio.

If you think about the section on how codecs work, you know that the codec looks at the audio waveform and determines, based on its knowledge of human hearing, what audio to remove that the ear cannot hear. The codec will first of all have a difficult time reproducing the clipped part of the waveform. Secondly, the clipping produces harmonics. If the codec is to make a decision on what audio to remove, it can very easily accidentally remove the audio that should remain in the waveform rather than removing the harmonics generated by clipping. This results in unexpected audio artifacts, usually unpleasant. This is why it is important not to hard clip the audio on the HD Radio digital audio channels.

One mistake stations make, particularly FM stations because the digital audio is very close to the sound of the analog audio, is that they attempt to

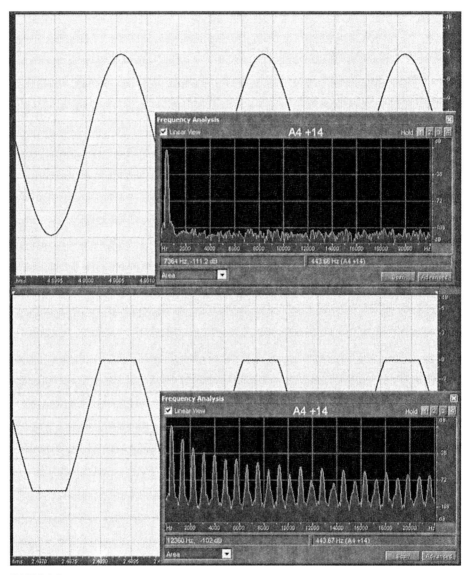

FIGURE 4-2

The effects of clipping on the spectral content of an audio signal. The audio sine wave is a 400-Hz tone. In the top screen shot, notice the spectral content in the lower right-hand corner. You can see the fundamental frequency. Anything else is in the noise floor. In the bottom screen shot, the sine wave was clipped five decibels. Note the significant harmonics generated by this clipping action. The perceptual codec may accidentally mistake these harmonics for valid audio, removing audio that is relevant, thus causing unpleasant artifacts. This is the reason clipping on the digital audio should be avoided.

process the digital audio exactly as the analog. The purpose of HD Radio technology is to give the listener a better experience. If your analog signal is already over processed, it will serve no purpose to over process the HD Radio digital audio channel. A little processing goes a long way on the digital audio. The codec will have a difficult time data reducing heavily processed audio, and it may result in unintended consequences. Make no mistake: audio processing, while one of the tools radio stations use to attract listeners, is technically distorting the audio. Start your processing adjustments with small amounts of processing, and gradually increase. You will find that a small change in, say, compression levels will result in a large change in the sound of the HD Radio digital audio.

For FM stations, the analog audio will be frequency limited to 15 kHz, processed and pre-emphasized, clipped, and then passed through a stereo generator. The digital audio, on the other hand, has an upper frequency limit of 20 kHz, will be processed, soft limited, and passed through the HDC codec. Both audio paths are extremely different from one another. If you try to set the processing on the digital side as it is set on the analog side, the digital audio will sound pretty raunchy.

When you achieve the sound you are looking for, you will need to make sure that the delay is adjusted correctly so that, when the HD Radio receiver blends, the transition is smooth and not disjointed. There are several methods to do this, one involving simply splitting the audio so that the analog audio is on one channel and the digital audio is on the other channel, and listening carefully with a pair of headphones. Another method involves recording a small portion of the audio on a digital editor using an HD Radio receiver to split the channels. You can then determine, by looking at the received analog and digital audio waveforms on the editor, how much your delay is off in nanoseconds and adjust accordingly.

You also want to balance the audio levels between the analog and digital channels. First, set up your analog modulation so that it is legal and where you want it to be. Then listen to the audio in split channel mode, and adjust the digital audio level. You want to bring the digital audio level to that of the analog audio. You do not want to adjust the analog level once you have set it. Once you think you have the levels set correctly, let the radio blend as it normally would. You should hear very little difference in level between the analog and digital audio if you have the levels set correctly.

Experiment with your new processor. You may be quite surprised to discover how much loudness you can get on an HD Radio digital-audio channel without over processing the audio and without using clipping. You will also need to get used to not hearing your adjustments in real time! Don't forget, there is greater than an eight-second delay on both AM and FM HD Radio systems. If you are like me, you will need to learn the virtues of patience with processing adjustments in the HD Radio world.

4.3 Feeding the processor

The HD Radio equipment will need an AES-3 signal as its input. The processors, however, give you an option to feed them from an analog source or an AES-3 source. Many of the processors have an automatic failover selection so that if the AES-3 input fails, it will default to the analog input.

If your studio and STL system can give you an AES-3 signal, by all means use it. If you are going to use analog signals to feed the processor, you may wish to use an A-to-D converter to convert these to AES-3 signals. The reason for this is that I have seen a processor fail and shut down its AES-3 outputs after a power bump because it did not have an AES-3 clocking signal available to it. Converting your analog audio to AES-3 will present your processor with this clocking signal and help prevent mishaps like this.

Some manufacturers make processors that combine the analog channel processing and the HD Radio digital audio processing into one chassis. I use an Omnia 5-EX on WOR with excellent results. There are also separate processors made for analog and digital. The choice is yours. Some feel that using an "all in one" processor is putting all of one's eggs into one basket and consequently not the best approach.

While it may sound odd to have both the analog and digital audio channels processed in the same chassis, there is not much common to both audio chains. Normally, the audio is input to the processor and enters an automatic gain control (AGC) circuit. From here, the audio usually separates into the analog side and the digital side. The "all in one" processors work extremely well.

If you intend on keeping your present analog processor for the analog channel, you will need to feed its output to the HD Radio equipment as an AES-3 signal. Contact the manufacturer of your processor regarding obtaining the AES-3 option. Alternately, you can use an external A-to-D converter.

Keep in mind that the newer audio processors, especially the processors used on the HD Radio digital audio channel, are computers. It is wise to put the audio processors on an uninterruptible power supply (UPS). In this way, a momentary power failure will not cause you to be off the air waiting for the audio processor to reboot.

4.4 The analog audio delay

There are several ways to implement and control the delay of the analog audio channel. One is to simply let the HD Radio exciter or Exporter add the necessary delay. This, actually, is the most common option with AM

HD Radio, though at least one processor manufacturer now gives you the ability to let the processor do this.

Most of the FM HD Radio processors that are "all in one" processors can produce the delay for the analog channel. This, in my opinion, is the preferred choice, since if you are using the HD Radio Exporter to create the required delay in the analog channel and the Exporter fails, your analog channel fails, too. In other words, using the audio processor to create the delay protects the analog channel from Exporter failure. The audio processors are very stable and can easily handle this chore.

A third method would be to use an external delay unit on the analog AES-3 signal to the transmitter. Eventide makes an excellent unit that can be adjusted to nanoseconds and will easily produce the analog channel delay for you. Of course, using this method, you may have one more thing to reboot in the event of failure. But the choice is yours.

4.5 **Where, physically, does the processor go?**

There are many schools of thought as to where the audio processor should physically be. With AM HD Radio, as of the writing of this book, the processor really must go at the transmitter site, unless you have two AES-3 audio channels between the studio and transmitter site. Putting the processor at the transmitter site simplifies adjustments for modulation but, of course, complicates matters for audio adjustments.

With FM HD Radio, the processor should be where the Exporter is. If your Exporter is located at the studio, the processor should be at the studio with it. My personal preference is to put the Exporter at the studio. As of this writing, the Exporter runs under the Microsoft Windows operating system. At some point, it will need to be rebooted, and this will happen at a most inopportune time. Having the Exporter at the studio makes it easy to reboot, and makes it easy to control or make changes to should the need arise.

If you are doing the FM analog audio delay in the audio processor or with an external delay device, the analog AES-3 signal feeds directly into the digital STL. At the transmitter site, the AES-3 signal of the analog audio feeds the exciter directly. The HD Radio AES-3 signal feeds the Exporter. The Exporter feeds the digital STL via Ethernet connection.

If you are doing the analog audio delay in the Exporter, the analog AES-3 signal from the audio processor is input to the Exporter, and the analog AES-3 output of the Exporter feeds the STL.

We will discuss the HD Radio equipment involved and how to connect it in a later chapter.

Installing AM HD Radio and Making it Work

5

5.1 Getting started with AM HD Radio

While, in a general sense, installing the HD Radio equipment at the AM transmitter is a fairly simple process, there are requirements that the transmitter and antenna system must meet. There are hardware options that you should strongly consider. A spectrum analyzer is required, and it must be set up in a specific manner to correctly adjust the HD Radio transmission system. This chapter will discuss all of this and help you get your HD Radio signal on the air by providing a complete description of the process.

Most of my experience is with an original iBiquity Digital Corporation exciter and with the Harris DexStar™ exciter. Many of my setup references in this chapter will be references from the DexStar. Read through this chapter, and compare the DexStar references to the manual on your exciter. Many descriptions are the same; some will be slightly different, as the manufacturers have the flexibility to manipulate the graphical user interface (GUI) of the system.

In addition to the HD Radio transmission equipment, you will need the proper licensing agreement from iBiquity Digital Corporation to operate your main HD Radio channel. The license for the main HD Radio channel is a one-time payment. Contrary to what you may have heard, there is no "perpetual" fee to operate your main HD Radio channel. If you intend to operate multicast channels (if that option becomes available for AM HD Radio) or sell utilization of your available data channels, iBiquity Digital Corporation does have a quarterly payment schedule for these additional services. Please consult with iBiquity Digital Corporation for specifics.

5.2 Internet access and IP ability

While not completely vital to the operation of the exciter at this point in time, you should consider having Internet access installed at the transmitter facility. Whether it is a dedicated DSL, or you bring it in via microwave or through the T1 you are using to bring audio to the site, is irrelevant. Having the largest "pipe" available coming into the site is not relevant, either. It is important that the Internet access is always on.

Later on, as we're setting up the exciter and getting the HD Radio signal on the station, you will see where Internet access comes into play. Briefly, having Internet access at the site will allow you to get into the exciter remotely to assess a possible situation. I have been able to get into an exciter, spot an error in the process of starting, and reboot the exciter before it had a chance to crash and take the station off the air.

You will also probably wish to run various data, for example, PAD (such as song title and artist) to your exciter. This can be done in many ways, but an IP connection is the easiest. And because your audio processing will be at the transmitter, being able to get into the processor from outside the transmitter facility via IP would be a great aid in fine-tuning the processing.

5.2.1 IP connectivity

IP connectivity to the transmitter site is important from two aspects. First, it will allow you to control the exciter from another location, such as your desk. Second, it is the preferred way to get PAD into the exciter.

IP connectivity can be through the Internet, over your bidirectional STL, through the use of a spread-spectrum IP radio, or through dedicated T1 service.

In parts of this chapter, you will see reference made to IP ports. Each IP connection is divided into 65,535 separate data channels, called ports. It is these multiple ports that allow your computer to perform several tasks at once, for example, checking your e-mail while you surf the Internet.

Some specific ports are commonly assigned for certain duties. For example, connection to a Web site is typically through port 80. E-mail normally comes into your computer on port 110 and goes out on port 25. Depending on how your system is configured, you may need to open up certain ports to the outside world on your router. It is recommended that the Internet not be connected "naked" to your HD Radio equipment, but that it have, at a minimum, a router installed to protect the equipment from an Internet hacker.

If, for example, you will be bringing PAD into the system through an Internet connection, it would be wise to have a router on this connection as a point of defense against a hacker getting into your equipment. Because the router acts like a traffic cop stopping unauthorized entry, you will need to open up specific ports on the router so that outside traffic on these ports is allowed in.

If your company does not have an IT department, you should probably obtain a book such as "Networking for Dummies," which will explain these topics more fully. Knowing how to handle the IT aspects of the HD Radio equipment will make your job much easier.

5.3 **Environmental requirements**

Most transmitter facilities are "out of sight, out of mind" places. They are usually just adequate for the job of housing the station's transmitter and associated equipment. Many are poorly ventilated, and the ventilation is rarely filtered. Many building interiors are subject to temperature variations down to freezing in the winter and above 100 degrees Fahrenheit (°F) in the summer.

The HD Radio exciter is a computer, as is the audio processor and the peripheral equipment. Consideration must be given to treating the exciter properly. This will help prevent lockups and help prevent the exciter from malfunctioning due to overheating.

This quote comes from the Harris DexStar manual:

> *Clean air is required. No salt air, polluted air, or sulfur air can be tolerated. A closed air system is recommended in these environments; that is, an air-conditioned room that recirculates and properly filters the room air. No outside air is to be brought into the transmitter room.*

Obviously, they feel strongly about this topic.

It is strongly suggested that the transmitter building or, at the very least, the area where the audio processing and HD Radio exciter is housed be air-conditioned in the summer and heated in the winter. Keeping the room above 60 °F in the winter and under 80 °F in the summer will help keep the HD Radio equipment operating correctly. Additionally, the equipment rack where the HD Radio equipment is housed should be equipped to move air through the rack.

It is as important as the temperature of the air in the room that the air be kept moving over heat-generating components. The idea is to constantly move the generated heat away from the components. In this way, even though heat is being generated, it can be managed.

If you are not air conditioning the building, it is important to filter the outside air coming into the building. Dust and dirt on heat-generating surfaces acts like a blanket, holding the heat in. It is also important to keep the air filters, if any, on the HD Radio equipment clean.

Because of the computers involved and the fact that your transmitter will be putting out slightly higher power while transmitting an HD Radio signal, air conditioning is highly recommended, especially in warmer climates. If you are happy in the environment in the transmitter building, the HD Radio equipment will be happy. This will help to ensure that your HD Radio installation will operate well and remain stable.

5.4 Requirements of the AM transmitter

One of the first things that needs to be done is an evaluation of the AM transmitter that is intended to be used for the HD Radio signal. As opposed to the FM HD Radio system, the digital portion of the AM HD Radio signal is actually a part of the AM analog signal and portions of it amplitude modulate the main carrier.

FIGURE 5-1

The Harris 3DX50, 50 kW AM transmitter. Digitally modulated transmitters are generally HD Radio ready.

As a general rule, tube-type AM transmitters cannot be used to transmit an AM HD Radio signal. Plate-modulated AM transmitters will distort the HD Radio waveform and will not have sufficient carrier phase stability to correctly pass the phase-modulated component of the digital portion of the HD Radio signal. Pulse duration–modulated (PDM), pulse width–modulated (PWM), and multiphase PDM transmitters will most likely not have the proper audio bandwidth to pass the HD Radio waveform correctly, and may distort the waveform. It may be possible, however, to correctly pass the HD Radio waveform through a multiphase PDM transmitter if the switching or sampling frequency employed is greater than 150 kHz. Digitally modulated AM transmitters, such as the Harris 3DX50 shown in figure 5-1, as a general rule, will work properly with an AM HD Radio signal.

So the two basic tests, then, are:

- Is the transmitter RF path phase-stable? and;
- Is the modulator bandwidth at least 50 kHz?

You should check with the manufacturer of your transmitter for HD Radio transmission compatibility. Some manufacturers have modification kits for their transmitters to make them HD Radio compatible in a cost-efficient manner. If your transmitter cannot be made HD Radio compatible, it will need to be replaced.

5.5 Requirements of the AM antenna system

One interesting and funny thing about AM radio stations is that no two antenna systems are the same. I have seen stations with nine tower directionals that can transmit the HD Radio signal just fine. I have seen a nondirectional station, which uses a modified version of a Franklin antenna, not be able to transmit an HD Radio signal due to the narrowband nature of the antenna.

Regardless of your antenna system, you should perform a full impedance sweep over a frequency band ±30 kHz from carrier. The results of a typical impedance sweep are shown in figure 5-2. This sweep should be performed at the output of the transmitter. On the basis of this sweep, you will likely then need to phase rotate the load so that the appropriate load symmetry is presented to the final amplifier in the transmitter. Each transmitter brand is different, and the tuning network introduces a certain amount of phase shift to the signal. This will change the sideband Voltage Standing Wave Ratio (VSWR) as presented to the final amplifier. You should check with the manufacturer of your transmitter to obtain the proper phase rotation information.

First, your load ±5 kHz from carrier should be as flat as possible, preferably presenting no more than a 1:1.035 VSWR across this passband.

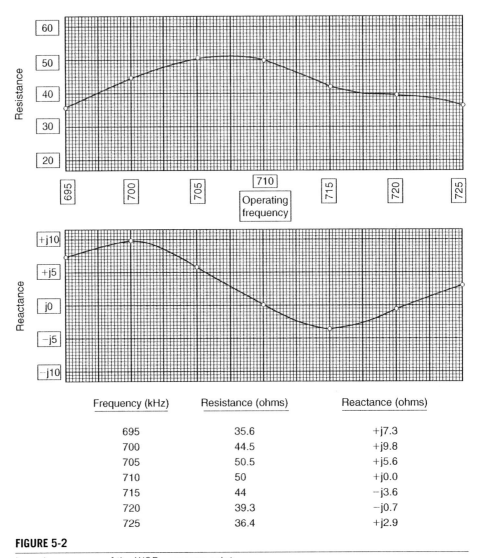

Frequency (kHz)	Resistance (ohms)	Reactance (ohms)
695	35.6	+j7.3
700	44.5	+j9.8
705	50.5	+j5.6
710	50	+j0.0
715	44	−j3.6
720	39.3	−j0.7
725	36.4	+j2.9

FIGURE 5-2

Impedance sweep of the WOR common point.

The resistances should be equal on both sides of carrier, and the reactances should be of equal magnitude but of opposite sign. This is called Hermetian symmetry.

The purpose of the Hermetian symmetry area is to ensure that the HD Radio Digital Subcarriers that are in quadrature with the analog AM signal are transmitted symmetrically. There have been reports of a "bacon frying" sound in the analog audio of some stations. Part of this can be attributed to some tilt in the impedance in the Hermetian area, and the upper and lower digital sideband subcarriers not properly canceling in "normal" (i.e., non-HD Radio) AM receivers.

You also need to achieve a VSWR no greater than 1.5:1 over a passband of ±15 kHz. Each sideband should be as identical as possible. In this way, the HD Radio waveform will pass through the antenna system with a

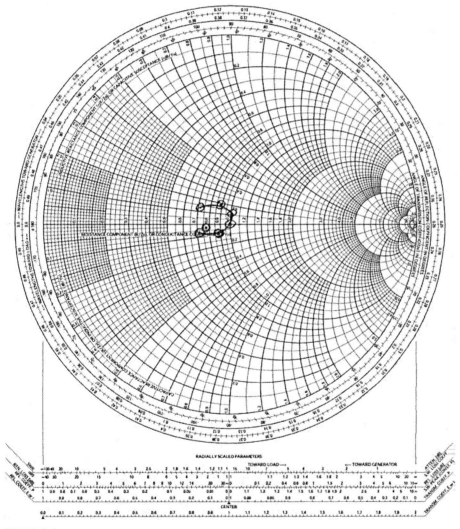

FIGURE 5-3

A Smith Chart of the antenna's impedance sweep is used to determine antenna input bandwidth and proper phase rotation of the load for the transmitter's final amplifier.

minimum of attenuation or distortion. A Smith Chart should be used to plot the load as shown in figure 5-3. You will then be able to tell if the load needs to be rotated in phase so that the correct VSWR range will be presented to the final amplifier.

If you find that your antenna does not have the abovementioned characteristics, you may need to call in an RF consultant. There are many tricks that can be used to flatten out the impedance. What will work and what it will cost are pretty much determined by the results of your initial tests. Deciding to try the HD Radio signal through your system even if you cannot meet the above is up to you. It may perform adequately. It may not. It doesn't hurt to try, though you may find that you cannot meet specifications for spectral regrowth, which will be discussed later in this chapter.

5.6 Installing the HD Radio equipment

First and foremost, the HD Radio exciter is a computer running the Linux operating system. While Linux is very stable and based on the UNIX operating system, there is a shutdown procedure Linux must go through, very much like that used by Microsoft Windows. It is strongly recommended that the HD Radio exciter be connected to power through an uninterruptible power supply (UPS), and that the UPS be connected to the exciter so that they talk to each other. In the event of a power failure, the exciter will stay up and will not crash. If there is no backup power available at the site, the exciter will shut down gracefully. This will prevent the corruption of files and the possibility that the station may be off the air for several minutes when power returns and the exciter reboots.

Next, be aware that a dual-trace oscilloscope and a spectrum analyzer are required for AM HD Radio installation. The oscilloscope should have a bandwidth of at least 50 MHz. The spectrum analyzer needs to be able to measure the AM broadcast band, and must be capable of a resolution bandwidth of 300 Hz. You should also have some type of HD Radio receiver available, one where you can split the analog audio off to the left channel, and the HD Radio digital audio off to the right channel (or vice versa) so they can be heard together. It would be preferable to use something like the Day Sequerra M4 or M2 monitors, or the Audemat-Aztec Goldeneagle HD AM. The radio is used to set the time delay between the digital and analog channels, and to assist in balancing audio levels between the analog and digital channels.

5.6.1 Connecting the HD Radio exciter to the transmitter

There are two signals that need to be inserted into the transmitter from the HD Radio exciter: the Magnitude signal and the Phase signal.

FIGURE 5-4

The Harris DexStar AM HD Radio exciter.

The Magnitude signal contains the analog AM audio, plus the HD Radio digital components that will amplitude modulate the transmitter. The Phase signal contains the station's carrier frequency, plus the phase-modulated components of the HD Radio digital signal. You should have a supply of 50-ohm coax with BNC connectors available.

First, you have a decision to make. If you connect the exciter directly to the transmitter, which would be the easiest method, the transmitter will be tied directly to the HD Radio equipment. If the HD Radio exciter fails, you would need to switch to a different transmitter to maintain service.

We think of an exciter, shown in figure 5-4, as a piece of RF gear that feeds the transmitter and that is what the HD Radio exciter is, with a twist. The exciter is a computer which runs the Linux operating system. Linux is very stable. But it is still a computer. Things happen. A hard drive could go bad, a memory module could go bad, and in that case the exciter will fail. Sometimes it just needs to be rebooted. You need a fail-safe plan.

If instead of using a direct connection you connect the Magnitude and Phase signals through a switching circuit, then when the HD Radio exciter fails, the transmitter's internal oscillator will switch in to drive the transmitter, and the audio processor's analog output will switch in to put audio back on the carrier. This is the preferred method of installation, as it provides you with a fail-safe method to stay on the air, with an analog-only signal, in the event of exciter failure.

There are two methods by which you can accomplish this feat. By far the easiest would be to use equipment supplied by the manufacturer of your exciter and transmitter, as shown in figure 5-5. It is intended to fully interface with the exciter, and not only monitors the exciter for failure, but also monitors the RF output of the exciter to not only keep the station on the air, but to protect output Metal Oxide Semiconductor Field Effect Transistors (MOSFETs) in the event of a loss of drive.

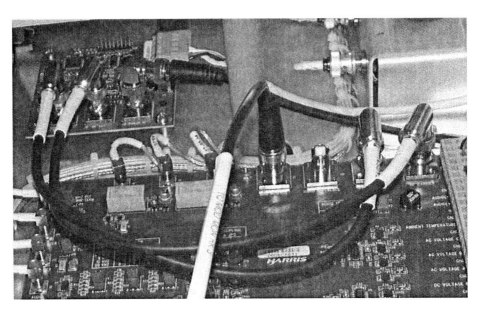

FIGURE 5-5

The RF switchboard supplied by the manufacturer is the best way to connect the RF from the HD Radio exciter to the transmitter. This particular board has RF sensing which will switch the system to analog operation automatically should the RF output of the exciter fail.

FIGURE 5-6

This is the relay used in WOR's old Harris DX-50 transmitter to switch between the internal oscillator in the transmitter and the RF from the HD Radio exciter.

The second method is to simply use a small signal relay, an example is shown in figure 5-6, and connect it to the HD Radio equipment so that it will place the exciter online when commanded by the system.

WOR uses Harris DexStar exciters. These exciters have a companion called an e-Pal, which can act as an AES distribution amplifier and a rate converter. It also monitors the exciter, and switches the audio in the event of an exciter failure. With its companion RF switching board which installs in the Harris 3DX50 transmitter used by WOR (figure 5-5), a failure of RF output from the exciter will cause the switchboard in the transmitter to switch to the internal oscillator to keep the transmitter on the air and forces the e-Pal to switch analog-only audio to the transmitter's input.

If you are using an older exciter or an exciter produced by another manufacturer, the e-Pal unit described above may be called an EASU (Exciter Auxiliary Services Unit). Some manufacturers build the EASU into the exciter. You will need to consult your manual and question the sales-person from whom you have purchased your HD Radio equipment.

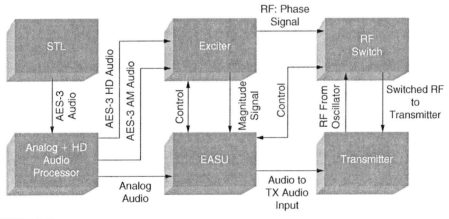

FIGURE 5-7

Block diagram of the AM HD Radio system showing how the equipment connects together.

The Magnitude output of the exciter connects to the EASU. The analog-only output of the audio processor also connects to the EASU. The EASU then feeds the audio input to the transmitter. Care must be taken to insure that the audio phasing is correct from the exciter to the transmitter's input. If you find that your positive peaks are in the wrong direction, you can always flip the audio over in the audio processor. Correct audio polar-ity is critical for proper reproduction of the HD Radio signal. You will not be able to null the "spectral regrowth" and your transmitter will produce out-of-band emissions if the polarity of the magnitude connection between the input of the transmitter and the exciter is incorrect.

The Phase output of the exciter connects to one input of the RF switch. The internal oscillator in the transmitter connects to other input of the RF switch. The output of the RF switch connects to the external RF input on the transmitter. Please refer to Fig. 5-7.

The AES signals from the audio processor connect to their appropriate inputs on the exciter: the analog output to the analog input of the exciter, the digital output to the exciter's digital input. Note that, in many cases, the AES-3 output of the audio processor, which contains the analog audio, is referred to as the analog output, while the analog audio input on the exciter is referred to as the analog input. This describes the content of the signal as being the analog audio. It does not mean that this is an analog signal: it is AES-3 data.

The non-AES-3 analog audio output of the audio processor then connects to the EASU to provide the transmitter with processed audio should the exciter fail.

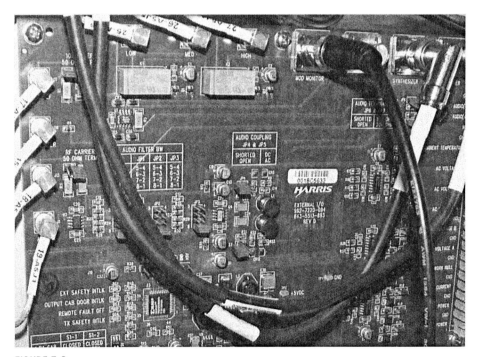

FIGURE 5-8

Any input filtering on the transmitter's audio input board must be bypassed. If possible, the audio input should be set for AC coupling.

Any connections between the RF switch and the EASU should be made at this time. Additionally, any connections between the exciter and the EASU should be made in addition to any connections between the RF switch and the exciter. You will need to refer to your manufacturer's literature. We will reserve connections to the station's remote control system until later.

You should consult the manufacturer of your transmitter regarding the audio input stages of the transmitter. Most AM transmitters have audio filtering to prevent out-of-band emissions. These filters must be removed before you can attempt to put an HD Radio signal on the air. Figure 5-8 shows the audio input board and filter jumpers of the Harris 3DX50 transmitter. The typical 12-kHz filters used will not only eliminate part of the HD Radio waveform, but also distort the phasing of the HD Radio subcarriers. If possible, you will want to set the audio input on the transmitter for AC coupling.

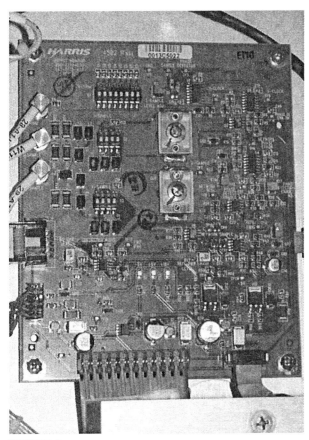

FIGURE 5-9

The output monitor of the transmitter may require adjustment to desensitize it to the HD Radio signal.

You should also consult with the transmitter manufacturer regarding the output monitor in your transmitter, see figure 5-9. All AM transmitters monitor the output for things such as VSWR and automatic power control. If the output monitor is too sensitive, it may mistake the HD Radio waveform as carrier pinch off and/or a VSWR condition, and will momentarily kill the output of the transmitter. This is annoying on the analog audio channel, as the audio will have pops in it. It can be devastating to the digital audio channel, as the radio will not have time to lock onto a stable digital subcarrier. You may find that, after making the initial adjustments on reduced power, you may need to spend time calming down and readjusting the transmitter's output monitor.

5.6.2 **Connecting the GPS**

The HD Radio exciter comes with a Global Positioning System (GPS) antenna. The GPS data provides the exciter with a highly accurate timing reference plus location information. Having your exciter GPS locked will also ensure carrier frequency stability, which will help listener's HD Radio receivers lock onto the various HD Radio stations in any given city faster. In the future, it may be possible to transmit the correct time to listener's radios. The GPS antenna needs to be mounted somewhere outside the transmitter building, perhaps on an STL antenna mount, (see figure 5-10) and its coax cable connected to the exciter.

The HD Radio exciter is designed to work with GPS data. It is strongly suggested that you provide this connection so the exciter does not lock up. If you find that for some reason you cannot connect the GPS antenna, it is possible to tell the exciter that it does not have a GPS antenna associated with it. However, it is best to have the GPS antenna connected and the GPS service activated in the exciter.

It is interesting to note that you can use either 50-ohm or 75-ohm cable should you need to extend the length of the coax that comes with the exciter's GPS antenna. Just make sure to calculate the delay caused by the length of cable you use (this information is in the exciter's manual), as you will enter this figure into the exciter's configuration later.

5.6.3 **Preliminary checks**

Next, before you boot up the exciter, make sure the output of the transmitter is terminated into a dummy load. You should not put the transmitter on the air and make adjustments unless it is absolutely necessary to do so, as chances are very good that you will initially produce out-of-band emissions. If you need to perform your initial adjustments into the antenna system, you should probably perform them after midnight.

FIGURE 5-10

The supplied GPS antenna needs to be placed where it has a good view of the sky, such as on the station's STL tower.

First, you will want to make sure that your switching unit is working correctly. With the exciter off, you will want to use an oscilloscope to check for analog audio at the input to the transmitter. With the exciter off, the EASU will sense the failure and should present the transmitter with the analog audio input. If this is not the case, you should troubleshoot and find the problem.

You should also, at this time, check to make sure that, with the exciter off, the transmitter's internal oscillator is connected to the transmitter's external RF input through the RF switch. This can be done by disconnecting the BNC plugs to and from the transmitter and measuring with an ohmmeter, (see figure 5-11) as a start, if you are using a simple relay switch. If you are using an interface from the transmitter's manufacturer, you can use an oscilloscope to see if an RF signal is present. The transmitter's power output should be ramped down to zero for this test. Once you are sure you have continuity from the oscillator to the external RF input, you can reconnect the plugs and consider bringing the transmitter up. The purpose of this test is to make sure you will have RF going to the transmitter's amplifier. If you attempt to bring the transmitter up, and the underdrive sensing circuit fails with no RF present, you may find yourself with many burned up MOSFETs.

FIGURE 5-11

Checking the RF switch's continuity with a multimeter.

You will need to use an oscilloscope to measure the level of the RF signal being supplied by the oscillator circuit in the transmitter. Some transmitters have the oscillator active while the transmitter is off (see figure 5-12). If so, use the oscilloscope to measure the peak-to-peak RF voltage with the oscillator connected to the transmitter's external RF input. The external RF input will present a load, usually 50 ohms, to the incoming signal. You need to measure this voltage with the load, not open circuit.

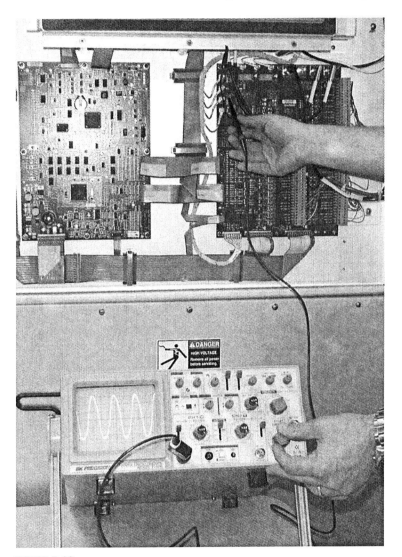

FIGURE 5-12

It is important to check the peak-to-peak RF voltage being delivered to the transmitter by the transmitter's internal oscillator and then match the output of the HD Radio exciter to the same level.

Turn the transmitter on briefly and make sure the peak-to-peak RF voltage does not change with the transmitter on. Write down this peak-to-peak level. You should also make note of and write down the power amplifier (PA) drive indication on the transmitter for comparison with the HD Radio equipment in line.

5.6.4 Initial boot up of the exciter and initial setup

You should now turn the HD Radio exciter on. It will take a short while to boot up. Let it fully boot. You will be fully booted when the GUI comes up and is no longer presenting you with booting messages. Do not be concerned that the GPS is unlocked at this time. It will take a few minutes for the GPS signal to lock under a normal boot up. Since this is the first time you have booted up this exciter in this location, it could take as long as 15 minutes. The GPS signal will eventually lock.

From this point on, you will see certain system commands listed in italics type. The commands listed in this chapter are based on irss version 2.3.3, operating system version 7.1, and operating system kernel 2.4.20–22 of the iBiquity Digital Corporation HD Radio software.

You first need to check the screen to make sure the exciter is operating on the correct band at the correct frequency. Locate the carrier frequency and make sure it is set to your station's frequency. If it is not, you will need to navigate to the *System Setup* area of the GUI and reset the band and frequency. This will force a reboot of the exciter. You will need to enter the password of the exciter to access the setup areas. Refer to your exciter's manual to get the default password. It is usually 1234, or 123456.

The exciter has a touch screen. Touch the *Password Block*, and a virtual keyboard will appear on the screen (see figure 5-13). Enter the default password, then hit the virtual *ENTER* key.

If you are the only person who has access to the exciter, you do not need to change the default password. If, however, the exciter is accessible by many people, it is a good idea to change the password so that curious fingers do not change the system settings, possibly taking the station off the air or causing the transmitter to emit out-of-band products. You will note that there is a button near the password entry field that will allow you to change the password. If you do change the password, make sure it is something you will not forget.

If you needed to change the carrier frequency, the exciter will prompt you for a reboot. Note that the exciter needs to be rebooted for this change to take effect. Select *YES* to allow the exciter to reboot.

5.6.5 Setting the GPS parameters

Navigate to the *System* screen, then to the *Network GPS* screen, and then to the *GPS Configuration* screen. Enter the delay, in nanoseconds, that

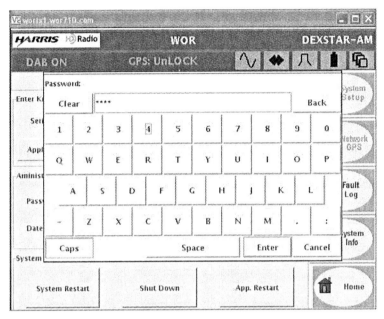

FIGURE 5-13

Password entry is made through a virtual keyboard on the exciter's touch screen.

you calculated for the length and type of cable you are using for the GPS antenna into the *Antenna Delay* field. This information can be found in the exciter's manual. Select your *Time Zone*, and select *Daylight Saving Time* if your area observes Daylight Saving Time. If there is a check box for **GPS Time Synch**, it should be checked.

5.6.6 Setting network parameters

Once the exciter is on the correct frequency, one of the first things you should do is set up the networking parameters. This can be found under the *System* menu as *Network Configuration*. Some manufacturers, like Broadcast Electronics, have a procedure to set networking parameters that require you to go to a Linux command line for setup. Consult your manual.

The first thing in this list is the *Hostname*, the networking name of the exciter. I used "wortx1" and "wortx2" as the hostnames for the two exciters that I have. *DO NOT* enter a space or other illegal character into the hostname field. Doing so will cause the exciter, on next reboot, to go into a reboot loop that you will not be able to escape out of. In this case, you will most likely end up sending the exciter back to the factory, as the manufacturers are under contract not to give out the root password for exciters. I know that as of the writing of this book, Harris has instituted a warning screen that catches illegal characters and warns you to change what you have input effective after irss version 2.2.5. Generally, any letter or number, and a dash (-) or underline (_) is acceptable.

The next field is the *Domain* field. It is OK to leave this field as it is, unless you will be connecting the exciter to a LAN that uses a domain server. If your LAN uses a domain server, you should enter the correct domain name in this field.

There is a row of buttons at the bottom of the Network Configuration screen. If you will be sending the exciter PAD via Ethernet, you should select the *Static IP* button and assign the exciter a static IP address. This is true also if you intend to utilize Virtual Network Computing (VNC) to get into the exciter remotely. VNC will be discussed later. If you will not be using a Static IP address, you can select Dynamic Host Configuration Protocol (*DHCP*) and the exciter will be assigned an IP address from your DHCP server. If your exciter will not be on a LAN, you can select *Off Net*.

If you have chosen to assign your exciter an IP address, you will need to enter the *IP address*, the *subnet mask* used on your LAN, and the Internet *gateway* address. If you do not know these items, you should get the information from your company IT department.

Depending on the software version that is running on the exciter, you may also see two fields called *Exciter Link* and *Exciter MAC*. These fields are used in FM Exporter systems and are not used for AM HD Radio exciters. *Exciter Link* will display a grayed out "local host" IP address of 127.0.0.1. *Exciter MAC* will be blank.

When you have entered all the information, and double-checked to make sure you do not have a space in the hostname field, you should select the *Save Cfg* button. The information will be saved, and you will be prompted to reboot the exciter.

Once the exciter has rebooted, you should go to the *Mode Control* screen, and turn the *Digital Subcarriers* off. You will find a virtual button to do this on the *Mode Control* screen.

5.6.7 Setting the RF output level of the exciter

If you are using an EASU, you should now place the system into Operate mode. Older EASUs have a rocker switch that needs to be switched to the Operate position. The newer EASUs, like the Harris e-Pal, have a push button. Once the system has been placed in Operate mode, if your EASU has an operational indication, it will be lit.

Take your oscilloscope and measure the RF level at the output of the RF switch. To make sure you are seeing RF from the exciter, momentarily disconnect the cable coming from the internal oscillator of the transmitter. If the RF goes away, your RF switch did not switch to the output of the exciter, and you will need to troubleshoot this. You want to be sure you are looking at the RF coming from the exciter.

Compare the peak-to-peak voltage measurement of the RF from the exciter with the measurement you made with the transmitter connected to its internal oscillator. If the RF from the exciter is higher or lower than what was coming from the transmitter's internal oscillator, you will need to adjust the *RF output* of the exciter.

The *RF output* adjustment may be in different locations depending on the manufacturer. It may be on the Digital Upconverter (DUC) board in the exciter, it may be on the RF switching interface installed in the transmitter, or it may be on the back of the exciter (see figure 5-14). Refer to your exciter's manual to determine where is the exciter's *RF output* adjustment.

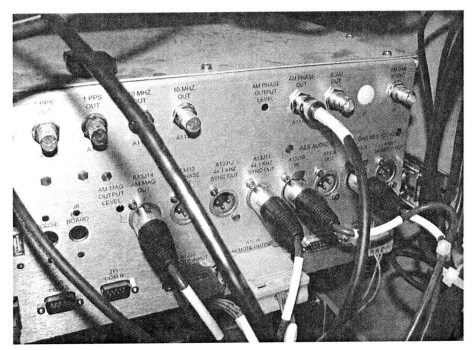

FIGURE 5-14

In the case of the DexStar, the RF level adjustment, sometimes called the Phase Level, is on the back of the exciter.

Move the oscilloscope into a position where you can observe the RF level at the output of the switchboard, and adjust the output of the exciter to the same peak-to-peak output the transmitter sees from its internal oscillator. Once this is done, you should switch between the internal oscillator and the HD Radio exciter to make sure the RF level seen by the transmitter does not change.

5.6.8 Setting the analog audio bandwidth

Go back to the exciter, and navigate to the *AM System Setup* screen (see figure 5-15). Make sure the *Analog Modulation* virtual button is *On*. You will also need to make a decision. The audio bandwidth of the analog audio can be set in the audio processor, or you can allow the HD Radio exciter to perform the audio bandwidth reduction. I prefer to have the audio processor do the bandwidth reduction. Very simply, the audio processor is designed to perform the audio roll off gracefully and it will sound good. The audio filter in the exciter is designed to protect the HD Radio subcarriers. I do not like the sound of it, as it is rather harsh.

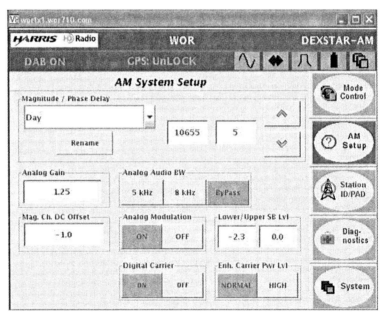

FIGURE 5-15

It is important to tell the exciter what bandwidth mode it will be operating in, as the exciter will instruct the radio how to handle incoming data.

If you are letting the audio processor handle the audio bandwidth reduction, set the *Analog Audio BW* setting to *Bypass* by pressing the *Bypass* virtual button. By default, setting the *Analog Audio BW* on the exciter to *Bypass* tells the exciter to operate in the 5-kHz transmit mode. You cannot run the audio processor with a bandwidth of 8 kHz in this mode – the excess audio bandwidth will interfere with the HD Radio subcarriers, and the radios will be told by the exciter that it is operating in 5-kHz mode (see figure 5-16). If you intend to operate with an audio bandwidth of 8 kHz, you will need to press the *8-kHz* button. Once you have made your selection, leave the exciter on this screen. We will be working with it shortly.

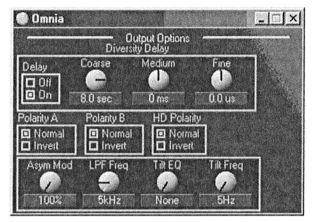

FIGURE 5-16

You will need to set the bandwidth of the audio processor if you select "bypass" as the bandwidth mode on the exciter.

5.6.9 Setting the analog audio level into the exciter

Next, we are going to set the audio level into the exciter for the analog channel. The exciter builds the entire AM HD Radio waveform internally, much in the same way the AM stereo exciters did in the 1980s, for reference purposes. We need to input a tone to the exciter and set the internal modulation level.

On the *Mode Control* screen of the exciter's GUI, press the *Digital Carrier OFF* button. You do not want the HD Radio subcarriers to appear for adjustment at this time – we are only looking for analog audio modulation levels.

Set the audio processor to produce a test tone, and set the AM output level of the processor to −3 dBFS (decibels full scale). If your audio processor does not have the ability to send a test tone, you will need a good audio test set, such as the Audio Precision test set, with an AES-3 output.

You could send an analog tone from a test set through an A-to-D converter. The tone frequency can be 400 Hz or 1 kHz, set to −3 dBFS.

On the back of the exciter, you will find a BNC connector labeled *AM Out*. Connect the *AM Out* of the exciter to the input of your oscilloscope. Set the oscilloscope so that you can observe a modulated AM carrier. With the tone output of the audio processor set to −3 dBFS, you should observe 95 percent AM modulation (see figure 5-17). The negative modulation envelope should not be cut off. If you do not see 95 percent negative modulation, you will need to make an adjustment on the exciter.

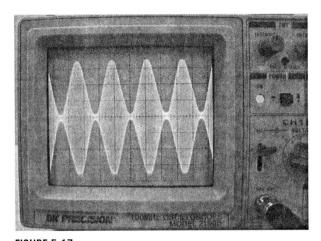

FIGURE 5-17

Set the internal modulation of the exciter to 95 percent.

If you do not see 95 percent modulation, go to the *AM System Setup* screen on the exciter and make small adjustments to the *Analog Gain* setting. Touch the *Analog Gain* block, and the virtual keyboard will appear. The default setting is 1.0. If you need to increase the modulation, enter in 1.1 and see where that takes you. If you need less modulation, enter in 0.9 and see where you end up. Once you have achieved 95 percent modulation, it is time to set the audio level into the transmitter.

5.6.10 Setting the audio level into the transmitter

Bring the transmitter up into the dummy load running on the RF from the HD Radio exciter. The transmitter will be up for a while, so set it to a relatively low level, say, one-quarter power.

Take a DC voltmeter, and measure the DC voltage across the audio input to the transmitter (see figure 5-18). It should be zero volts. If it is not, you will need to adjust the *DC Offset* setting in the *AM System Setup* screen of the exciter to produce zero volts DC at the input to the transmitter. The normal setting for *DC Offset* is −1.0.

Once you have obtained zero-volts DC at the input to the transmitter, check the modulation of the transmitter. It must match the 95 percent obtained when you measured the *AM Out* jack on the exciter. If it is not 95 percent, you will need to adjust the *AM Magnitude* pot most likely located on the back of the exciter.

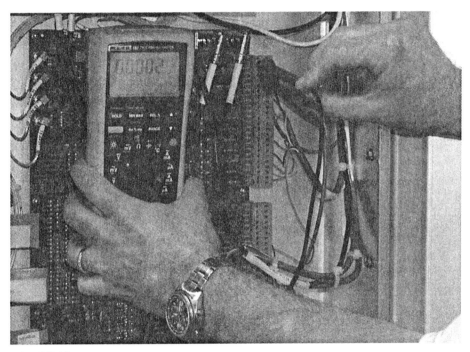

FIGURE 5-18

The DC offset into the transmitter should be zero volts.

Do not make any adjustments to the audio input level in the transmitter. The audio level to the transmitter *must* be adjusted at the exciter. Place the oscilloscope where it can easily be seen, and adjust the *AM Magnitude* pot to produce 95 percent modulation of the AM transmitter (see figure 5-19).

Once you have obtained 95 percent modulation on both the *AM Out* jack of the exciter and of the transmitter, you should increase transmitter power to full power output and reset the *AM Magnitude* pot on the exciter as necessary to obtain 95 percent modulation at full power. Then, shut off the test tone and modulate with program material, observing both

FIGURE 5-19

Use the *AM Magnitude* adjustment to set the modulation of the transmitter to 95 percent.

the *AM Out* jack of the exciter and the output of the transmitter. You should ensure that you are not hitting negative modulation peaks of any greater than 95 percent.

Carrier pinch off can do several things. First and foremost, if the carrier disappears, an HD Radio receiver will glitch as the incoming data will be disrupted. It will also cause false VSWR trips of the transmitter, and could, in extreme circumstances, cause damage to the transmitter, such as blown output MOSFETs. If you observe modulation greater than 95 percent, adjust the output of the audio processor to bring them to 95 percent negative. *Do not* adjust the *Magnitude* adjustment on the exciter to do this.

The correct adjustment of the *Magnitude* level into the transmitter is critical, as the primary HD Radio subcarriers are injected through the audio input of the transmitter. Once you see that the transmitter is producing 95 percent modulation with tone as the exciter does, you should not adjust the *AM Magnitude* pot on the exciter any longer. Return the transmitter to reduced power operation unless you are certain your dummy load will be able to function properly at full power with modulation for an extended period of time.

5.6.11 Setting the HD Radio subcarrier levels and adjusting for best performance

We are now ready to check the levels of the HD Radio subcarriers as well as make adjustments to bring the "spectral regrowth" and out-of-band emissions down to legal levels. You will need a spectrum analyzer for these adjustments (see figure 5-20). Not only will the spectrum analyzer need to be capable of measuring at the frequency of an AM station, but it will also need to be able to operate with 300-Hz resolution bandwidth. The spectrum analyzer will also need to be capable of running and displaying an average of at least 100 sweeps.

Before we connect the spectrum analyzer, it should be said that the biggest mistake people make when setting up their first AM HD Radio station is that they perform the next set of adjustments far too fast. This is going to take you several hours. It cannot be done in 10 minutes. The more time you spend making these adjustments, the better your HD Radio system will perform.

Connect the spectrum analyzer to the transmitter sample port through RF attenuators. When performing this adjustment, it is critical that the front end of the spectrum analyzer not be overdriven. This could cause false measurement of the spectral regrowth region, as an overdriven front end will produce harmonics and splatter that is not actually present, and it will be displayed on the analyzer as such. Note that when setting the input level of the spectrum analyzer, all signals present must be taken into account, not just carrier.

Once you are sure that the spectrum analyzer is not being overdriven, you need to set it up correctly. First, set the center frequency to your station's frequency. Set the span to 100 kHz, so that you are seeing ±50 kHz on each side of the carrier. Set the amplitude of the carrier so that it just

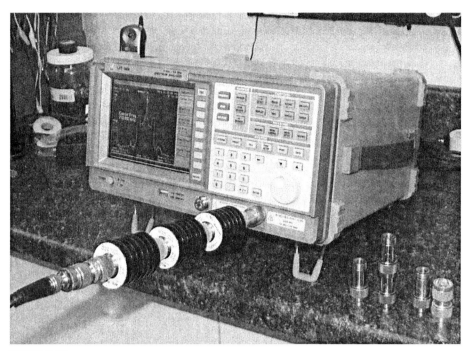

FIGURE 5-20

The spectrum analyzer is used to correctly adjust the system for the correct HD Radio waveform.

touches the top line of the graticule. You want at least 80 dB of measurement headroom. Set the resolution bandwidth to 300 Hz, and the video bandwidth to 1 kHz.

Refer to the manufacturer's instructions. They will indicate a starting point for the *Magnitude/Phase Delay* setting for your transmitter. Make sure the *Magnitude/Phase Delay* is set to the starting number as specified by the manufacturer.

Navigate to the *Mode Control* screen on the exciter's GUI, and turn the *Digital Carriers* on. Navigate back to the *AM System Setup* screen.

You may notice that your transmitter starts to hiss. This is normal and is nothing to be concerned about. You are simply hearing the HD Radio waveform from the transmitter the same way you hear the analog modulation ring in the tuning components. It is very disconcerting at first, as most of us associate this sound with either a pressure leak in a transmission line or with something arcing over. Nothing will burn up. This is a sound you will eventually get used to.

You should now see "shoulders" on your signal as displayed on the spectrum analyzer. You will also most likely be looking at a lot of "junk" on each side of the HD Radio waveform (see figure 5-21). In particular, you will most likely see large humps centered ±25 kHz, give or take, from carrier.

These humps are called spectral regrowth. They are an intermodulation product and reflection of the primary HD Radio carriers. The primary HD Radio carriers, remember, are located at 10–15 kHz from carrier. The spectral regrowth located −25 kHz from carrier is related to the upper HD Radio primary sideband. The spectral regrowth located +25 kHz from carrier is related to the lower HD Radio primary sideband.

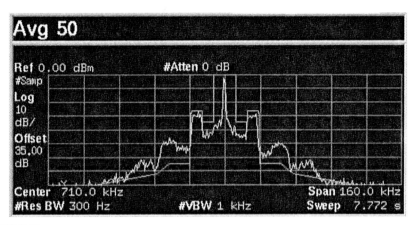

FIGURE 5-21

You may have a mess on the spectrum analyzer when you first bring the transmitter up. Adjusting the *Magnitude/Phase Delay* will bring the out-of-band products under control.

There are numerous things that cause these reflections, for example, modulator, PA, and antenna system bandwidth. The primary contributor to spectral regrowth tends to be the alignment of the magnitude and phase signals through the transmitter RF chain, which will cause intermodulation products if the modulator, PA, and antenna system bandwidth is not optimal. The tertiary and secondary HD Radio subcarriers phase modulate the carrier. The primary HD Radio subcarriers amplitude modulate the carrier. The timing of these portions of the HD Radio waveform must be correct or spectral regrowth develops.

First things first, however. Measure the level of the upper and lower HD Radio Primary sidebands at ±12.5 kHz. To do this, set the spectrum analyzer to average, and for now simply do an average of 30–40 sweeps. The level of the primary HD Radio carriers should be −28 dBc (−27.8 dBc is the maximum allowable) as referenced to carrier level. You may find this relatively easy to measure if you average, then set a marker on the carrier, and use a delta marker to measure the level of the HD Radio subcarriers.

If they are not -28 dBc, you can adjust them on the *AM System Setup* screen. Simply touch the number block in the area where it says *Lower/ Upper SB Level*. This number is in dB. If you need to bring the lower sideband down, say 1.2 dB, enter -1.2 on the virtual keyboard that comes up when you touch the *Lower SB Level* block. Restart the average on the analyzer and check to make sure your adjustment was correct. You want both HD Radio Primary sidebands equal in level at -28 dBc.

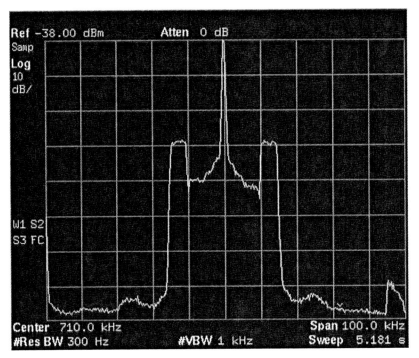

FIGURE 5-22

The correct HD Radio waveform after making the magnitude and phase adjustments.

We are next going to minimize the spectral regrowth. While the FCC mask says that we can have energy up to -35 dBc in this area, know that spectral regrowth is directly related to transmitted data errors. The higher the spectral regrowth, the more errors we are transmitting; the more errors in the signal, the less digital coverage your station will have. The idea is to minimize the reflections being caused, thereby minimizing the transmitted data errors. We are aiming for a number below -65 dBc, as this is the level called for in the NRSC-5 IBOC mask. Adjusting the timing and aligning the portions of the HD signal contained in the Magnitude and Phase signals will minimize the spectral regrowth.

Another reason to minimize spectral regrowth is to minimize interference to third adjacent stations. The spectral regrowth will appear as a hiss under a third adjacent signal. Minimizing the spectral regrowth as much as possible is being a good neighbor.

You will notice two blocks in the *Magnitude/Phase Delay* area of the *AM System Setup* screen. The block on the left is the *Magnitude/Phase Delay* adjustment. The block on the right is the amount that will be adjusted by pressing an *Up* or *Down* arrow. Set the right-hand block to 100 by pressing the block and entering it into the virtual keyboard.

Restart the averaging on the spectrum analyzer, set a marker on the carrier, and set a delta marker on either spectral regrowth hump, at either −25 or +25 kHz, or where the hump is highest. When the average is complete, read the delta marker and write this figure down so you don't forget it.

Go to the *AM System Setup* screen on the exciter and write down the *Magnitude/Phase* adjustment number next to the delta marker measurement on your notepad. This is your starting point. Press either the *Up* or *Down* arrow located in the *Magnitude/Phase Delay* area. Because we don't know which direction will make the spectral regrowth better, just pick a direction. When you hit that arrow, you will notice the *Magnitude/Phase* adjustment number changes by 100 in whichever direction you picked. Write this new number down on your notepad.

Restart the averaging on the spectrum analyzer. When the average is finished, reset your marker on carrier, read the delta marker on the spectral regrowth hump, and write it on your notepad next to the *Magnitude/Phase Delay* adjustment number you wrote down previously. The level of the delta marker will have gotten lower, higher, or not changed. If it has increased or not changed, we are going in the wrong direction with the *Magnitude/Phase Delay* adjustment. If it has decreased, we are going in the right direction. If we have gone in the wrong direction, go back to the exciter and hit the opposite arrow from the one you pressed last two times. If you are going in the correct direction, press the same arrow you pressed one time. Write the new *Magnitude/Phase Delay* adjustment number on your notepad.

Restart the averaging on the spectrum analyzer. When the average is finished, read the delta marker again. Keep repeating these steps until you find the place where the spectral regrowth appears to bottom out. You will notice with each adjustment that the spectral image of your signal keeps getting better (see figure 5-22).

Once you have found the apparent null in the spectral regrowth, you will need to reset your average to at least 100 traces on the spectrum analyzer, then let the analyzer average. This will take roughly 5–10 minutes.

At the end of the average, you will want to set a marker on carrier, and set a delta marker at −25, −12.5, +12.5, and +25 kHz. The readings obtained at ±12.5 kHz will be the level of the primary HD Radio subcarriers. If it is not −28 dBc, go to the exciter and reset the *Lower/Upper SB Level* adjustments. The markers at ±25 kHz are the spectral regrowth measurement. This is a coarse adjustment, as we were looking for it to bottom out and were adjusting by 100. We also were only averaging 40 times.

Write the measurements obtained by the delta markers at −25 and +25 kHz on your notepad, along with the *Magnitude/Phase Delay* adjustment number on the exciter. The adjustment range in the right-hand block is now set to 100. Set this number to 10. Select the *Up* or *Down* arrow and press the one you selected. The *Magnitude/Phase Delay* adjustment number will increase or decrease by 10. Write the new number down on your notepad. Restart the average on the spectrum analyzer. We will be doing 100 sweep averages from this point forward.

Once the average is complete, reset the marker on carrier and measure the delta markers at ±25 kHz again. Repeat the *Magnitude/Phase Delay* adjustment and reset the averaging steps until you have obtained the apparent null of the spectral regrowth.

We will not fine-adjust the spectral regrowth until we put the transmitter back on the antenna. The adjustment may change due to antenna bandwidth.

On the exciter, go to the *AM System Setup* screen and turn the *Analog Modulation* on. Note that you will not be able to accurately read analog modulation with the HD Radio subcarriers on. Your modulation monitor will indicate that you are overmodulating (see figure 5-23). This is normal. If you need to measure and set analog modulation, you will need to shut the HD Radio subcarriers off to do so. Turn the HD Radio subcarriers back on when you have completed adjusting the analog modulation. You will find the *Digital Carriers On/Off* buttons on the *Mode Control* screen.

FIGURE 5-23

When the HD Radio subcarriers are on, the modulation monitor will show apparent overmodulation. This is normal, as the monitor is responding to the extra energy caused by transmission of the HD Radio digital sidebands.

See how the transmitter is behaving while operating into the dummy load. If it seems stable, bring it up to full power. If the transmitter seems to glitch and/or back its power down, you will need to adjust the output monitor on the transmitter. Once the transmitter is stable, it is time to put it on the air at full power.

5.6.12 Putting the transmitter on the air and fine-tuning the spectral regrowth

Navigate to the *Mode Control* screen on the exciter and turn the *Digital Carriers* off. Put the transmitter on the air and measure the modulation on your modulation monitor. You want to adjust the AM output of the audio processor so that you are not exceeding 95 percent negative modulation peaks. Contrary to what you may have heard, you can modulate the transmitter with 125 percent positive modulation when you are running HD Radio. Most manufacturers say that you should adjust the positive peak control on the audio processor for 140 percent, as the exciter will limit the positive peaks. I set WOR's positive peaks on the processor to 125 percent and leave them there. I don't trust the clipping in the exciter, but the choice is yours.

Once you have your analog modulation set, go back to the *Mode Control* screen on the exciter and turn the digital carriers on. Let the transmitter sit with the HD Radio subcarriers on for a few minutes to make sure it is stable. You may find that you need to fine-tune the output monitor now that the transmitter is operating on the antenna. You may notice that your modulation monitor is indicating −100 percent modulation and high positive peaks. This is normal with the extra energy in the sidebands caused by the HD Radio subcarriers and is nothing to worry about. Your analog modulation did not increase and you are not overmodulating.

Once you are sure the transmitter is stable, recheck the carrier level on the spectrum analyzer and then set it to average at least 100 times. While you are waiting for the spectrum analyzer to average, go to the exciter and navigate back to the *AM System Setup* screen.

Once the analyzer has averaged, set a marker on carrier, and a delta marker on either spectral regrowth hump at −25 or +25 kHz. Measure the spectral regrowth. It should be close to the reading you obtained on the dummy load.

Reset the adjustment step for the *Magnitude/Phase Delay* on the exciter to 1. We will now fine-tune the spectral regrowth. Press either the *Up* or *Down* arrow, and write the new *Magnitude/Phase Delay* adjustment down. Reset the averaging on the spectrum analyzer. When the average is done, set your carrier marker and read your delta marker. Repeat to minimize the spectral regrowth, which should now be well below −65 dBc (see figure 5-24). You may need to do this several times to find the absolute minimum.

Once you have found the absolute null of the spectral regrowth, set delta markers again at ±12.5 kHz and measure the level of the primary HD Radio subcarriers. If they are not −28 dBc, make the appropriate adjustments on the *AM System Setup* screen. If you need to adjust the primary HD Radio subcarriers, you will need to average again and check to make sure the primary HD Radio subcarriers are where they belong.

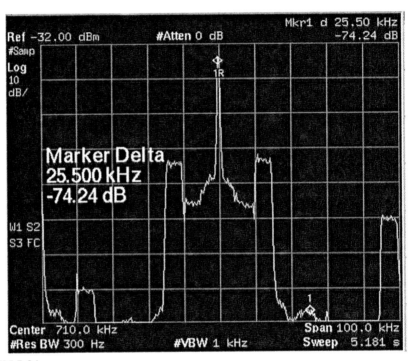

FIGURE 5-24

The HD Radio waveform showing a marker on the spectral regrowth. This was measured in the field at a location 2.3 miles from the transmitter site. The pieces of HD Radio waveform you see on the left and right are WFAN and WABC, respectively.

Once you have done this and are sure the system is correct, take a screen shot of the spectrum analyzer for your records. There are several ways to accomplish this depending on your spectrum analyzer. I prefer to save the screen shots to a flash drive and print them later from a photo-editing program. You may want to take several screen shots with the delta markers and their readings on the screen.

After you have taken a screen shot, reset the span on the spectrum analyzer for 200 kHz, reset the carrier level, and then restart the averaging again. When the average is complete, take a screen shot for your records. You may need to set a marker on carrier and delta markers on any significant bumps you may see on the display. This average will show complete compliance for mask purposes. If you have other stations nearby, they may appear on the analyzer if they are picked up through the antenna and seen at the transmitter's sample port (see figure 5-25). Make sure you know which stations they are so that you can identify them in your performance report.

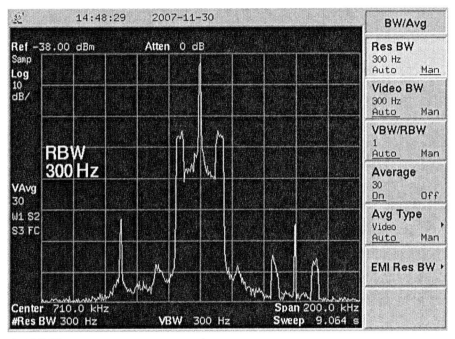

FIGURE 5-25

The 200 kHz span screen shot of the spectrum analyzer, looking at the WOR signal. WFAN is on the left of the WOR signal; WABC is on the right.

If you operate with separate antenna configurations day and night, you should perform the *Magnitude/Phase Delay* alignment again on the nighttime antenna. You can start with the final numbers you obtained going through the procedure the first time, and fine-tune from there. You can change to nighttime mode on the *AM System Setup* screen, then perform your *Magnitude/Phase Delay* adjustments to fine-tune the spectral regrowth null for the night antenna. Make sure to save the spectrum analyzer screen shots. You will need one at a span of 100 kHz, and another at a span of 200 kHz.

Once your system has been set up and the spectral regrowth has been minimized, you should take a set of spectral measurements in the field to make sure everything is okay. Many times, the monitor port on a transmitter will skew the measurements or may not show the signal as it will actually pass through the antenna. I have located a place approximately 2.3 miles in front of the WOR array that is clear of obstructions where we have a measured 1.5 volts per meter of signal (see figure 5-24).

The location you choose should be free of reradiating structures and, if you are directional, should be in the center of the main lobe of the signal. You will need to make and save spectral measurements with a span of 100 and 200 kHz for both day and night patterns, if this applies. If you find anything that looks incorrect, you may wish to make further adjustments to the exciter.

You may also, at this time, wish to take a spectral reading and save the measurement using the peak-hold feature of the spectrum analyzer rather than the averaging feature to prove compliance with the FCC regulation 73.44 as relates to allowable emissions. Note that this measurement should be at 200-kHz span, and that, because the peak values of the HD Radio subcarriers are higher than the average values, your primary HD subcarriers and spectral regrowth will appear higher. The idea of this measurement is to show full compliance with 73.44, not to adjust the HD Radio system.

You have now completed the RF alignment of your HD Radio system. You should print the screen shots you made after all of your adjustments were complete and write a report showing compliance with the FCC and NRSC-5 IBOC mask. This report should go into the station's files as annual performance measurements and compliance should the FCC wish to see it.

5.6.13 Adjusting the audio time delay

Next, you need to complete the audio alignment of your system. For this, you will need an HD Radio modulation monitor, such as the Day Sequerra M2 (see figure 5-26) or the Audemat-Aztec Goldeneagle HD AM. You can also use a car or home HD Radio receiver, but it must have the ability to split the analog and digital audio so that one stream is on the left channel and the other is on the right channel. You will also need a pair of headphones, as this is the easiest way to hear the delay correctly in the noisy transmitter room.

They say that a first impression is everything. It is extremely important that the time delay of the analog audio channel be as close as possible to the delay of the digital audio channel. If the first impression a listener has of your HD Radio signal is disjointed audio when his or her radio blends

FIGURE 5-26

The Day Sequerra M2 allows the audio to be split so that the analog audio signal can be heard on the left channel and the digital audio signal can be heard on the right channel. This helps simplify setting the time delay.

between analog and digital audio, they may not come back for a second listen.

On the exciter, navigate to the *Audio Setup* screen. Check to see if you are "ramped in" to delay on the analog channel. To check this, look in the *Ramp Control* section. It will list a *Final* and *Current* delay. If they are zero, you are not in delay.

Under *Delay Adjustment*, set the *New Delay* to 8.4 seconds. This will be a good starting point and should be very close to the final delay you need. Set the *Ramp Rate* to 100. If you wish, because you most likely want to get into delay quickly, you can set the ramp rate to a lower number, but if you are doing this in the middle of the afternoon, it will be highly noticeable on the air in the analog channel, as with the ramp rate set to 100, the system adds or subtracts one sample for each 100 samples. At a lower ramp rate, this addition or subtraction of samples becomes audible. Press the *Up* arrow under *Ramp Control*. You will see the *Current Delay* start to increment up. When this has reached 8.4 seconds, put the headphones on.

You will notice that the analog audio is on one channel, possibly the left, and the digital audio will be on the opposite side, possibly the right. Pay very close attention and see if you can tell if one is ahead of the other. You can easily change the delay time by changing the *New Delay* field under *Delay Adjustment* and walk it in. When you are finished, make sure the *Blend Control* on the exciter is set to *Enable Blending*, then set the radio or monitor back to normal mode. You should notice a quality change when the radio blends from analog to digital, but they should not be out of sync. The blend should be very smooth. You should also reset the *Ramp Rate* to 100 at this time if you changed it.

If you wish to get the timing between the channels as close as possible, you can set your radio or monitor to split mode and record both channels on a digital editor. You should then be able to measure the exact time delay between both the analog and digital streams, and make the adjustment on the exciter to make them exact.

You may wish to spend some time getting the digital audio channel to sound the way you want it to. Note that there will be an approximate 8.4-second delay from the time you make an adjustment on the processor until the time you hear it on the radio. You will find that this takes some getting used to.

You will also want to balance the levels between the analog and the digital audio channels so the blend will not have an abrupt level change. To do this, *do not* adjust the output of the processor for the analog channel. Adjust the output of the digital channel of the processor. Because your analog channel is the one most persons are listening to, and because it has modulation limits imposed by FCC regulation, let the analog channel be the standard. Adjust the levels of the digital channel to the analog channel, not the other way around.

Let the radio blend from analog to digital. Make your level adjustment on the digital output of the processor, wait 10 seconds, and then make the radio blend again. You may need to do this several times to get the levels exact.

5.6.14 Entering station-specific text information

Before you complete the setup and installation of the exciter, there are a few things left to input. Navigate to the *Station ID* screen on the exciter.

Do not attempt to change the frequency listed on this screen. This is your station's carrier frequency, and changing this will cause the exciter to operate on the wrong frequency.

FIGURE 5-27

Some HD Radio receivers will display the *Long Station Name SIS* data field. Make sure it is something you would want the public to see.

Under *Station Information*, enter the station's call letters where indicated. The station's call letters will appear on a listener's radio when they first tune to your station. The *Country Code* should be 1 for broadcasters in the United States. The *Network Code* should be what the manufacturer tells you it should be. The *Facility ID* should be your FCC facility ID as listed in the FCC database.

The *Long Station Name* field can be something like your corporate name or station's slogan see figure 5-27. WOR's says, "Real Talk Radio". The *Long Station Name* field will appear on some receivers, but not others, so don't put something off-color in this field as a joke. And do not leave it blank. This field *must* be filled. You will notice that Harris puts the serial number of your exciter in this field just to have something in there. Please don't transmit the serial number of your exciter. It looks ridiculous on a listener's radio.

5.6.15 Backing up your exciter's configuration

Once you have entered the *Station Information*, you should back up the configuration of the exciter in the event there is a problem, or you receive a software update. To do this, navigate to the *Upgrade* screen and insert the flash drive that came with your exciter into an available USB slot. You will most likely find the USB slots on the back of the exciter.

At this time, you should either shut the transmitter off or take the HD Radio system to nonoperational status. The next steps will force the exciter to reboot, which will glitch the transmitter.

On the *Upgrade* screen, you will see a *Save Cfg* button. Note and be forewarned that, once the configuration is saved, the exciter will reboot, most likely taking you off the air. Press the *Save Cfg* button. The exciter will prompt you to insert the flash drive into a USB port. Press the *OK* button, as you have already inserted a USB flash drive into a USB port. When the configuration is saved, the exciter will tell you it is finished. It will then warn you that pressing *OK* will force a reboot. Press *OK*. It may prompt you again for the reboot. Press *OK* if it does. Once the exciter reboots, remove the flash drive from the USB port and put it in a safe location in case it is needed.

The reason the exciter does this is that it is set up to save its configuration, then reboot to launch an update CD ROM. Because you are not updating the exciter, it will simply reboot.

You may wish to have a spare hard drive on the shelf. If the hard drive is starting to go bad, it will generally turn up during an update when the rebuilt operating system checks the integrity of the installed files. Note that any updates to the HD Radio software will normally rebuild the entire hard drive and operating system file structure, as well as install an updated operating system.

5.6.16 Remote controlling exciter functions

You will most likely want to connect the exciter to your remote control system. You should put the *HD Carriers On* and *Off* controls onto your remote control so that you can shut the HD Radio subcarriers off in the event of a problem. Likewise, you may want to connect the HD Radio system bypass controls to the remote control so that you could take the HD Radio equipment completely out of the system. I have had the analog side of the exciter lock up, so that 8 seconds of programming was stuck in a loop, repeating. Because the exciter was still putting out RF, and because the exciter did not send a failure command to the EASU, WOR sat there repeating itself. We were able to take the HD Radio system off the air and operate the transmitter in analog mode via remote control.

On the back of the exciter, you will find the remote input and output connectors. You will need to refer to the manual on your exciter. In many instances, you will find it far easier to connect to the remote input and output connectors if you break them out to either terminal strips or punch blocks. Most manufacturers have breakout methods available.

REMOTE_DIGITAL_ON and *REMOTE_DIGITAL_OFF* when taken momentarily to ground will turn the HD Radio subcarriers on and off. There is an HD Radio on status available as *DIGITAL_ON/OFF_OUT*.

To change mode for nighttime antenna, take *REMOTE_NIGHT* to ground momentarily; for the daytime antenna, use *REMOTE_DAY*. Status for these is available as *DAY/NIGHT*.

If you carry sports, or for other reasons, you may wish to have the ability to ramp down the time delay. This can be accomplished by taking *DIVERSITY_ DELAY_RAMP_UP* or *DIVERSITY_DELAY_RAMP_DOWN* momentarily to ground. With the *Ramp Rate* setting set to 100, it will take approximately 10 minutes to fully ramp into or out of delay.

5.6.17 Setting up IP control of the exciter

If you wish to have the ability to get into your exciter from another location, iBiquity Digital Corporation has put a program called Virtual Network Computing (VNC) into the exciter. VNC will put the exciter's GUI on your home or office computer. Note that the exciter needs to have a static IP address for you to use VNC.

VNC can be used in two ways. One way is to download VNC from http://www.realvnc.com. If you do not want to do this, or if you go some place and VNC is not installed on a computer at this location, the exciter can download a Java version of VNC to the computer.

VNC Viewer : Authentication [No Encryption]

Username: [   ] [OK]

Password: [|] [Cancel]

FIGURE 5-28

The VNC login block.

You will first need to configure a VNC password on your exciter. To do so, navigate to the *Mode Control* screen. Here, you will find a button that says *Change VNC Password*. Change the password to something you can easily remember. Note that this password will not be saved on the flash drive on which you saved the exciter's configuration. If you upgrade the exciter's software, you will need to reenter your password for VNC. The default password is "password."

You will need to configure your Internet router to open ports 5810 and 5910 for TCP to the IP address of the exciter, in addition to port 80 if you

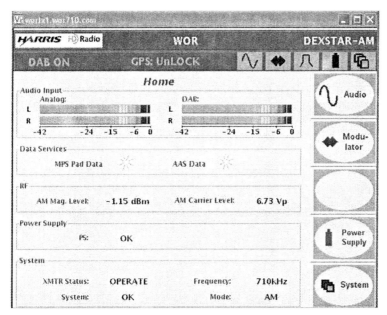

FIGURE 5-29

Using VNC is like sitting in front of the exciter.

intend to use the Java version of VNC. You only need to open port 5910 if you will be using the downloaded version of VNC exclusively.

If you have downloaded VNC to your computer, you would open VNC and connect to the Internet IP address at your exciter's location followed by :5910. If my IP address at the transmitter site is 10.1.1.27, I would enter 10.1.1.27:5910 into the VNC connection screen. If I were going to use Internet Explorer to download the Java version of VNC from the exciter, I would enter into the address bar: http://10.1.1.27. A VNC splash screen appears, VNC loads from the exciter, and it will display the IP address of the exciter appended by :10; the exciter's Java VNC assumes that the first two digits of the IP port number are 59. Clicking OK will make it ask for your password (see figure 5-28). Enter your password and you will be into the exciter.

Once you have logged in with VNC, it is almost the same as sitting in front of the exciter (see figure 5-29). Just be careful, as you can change something that might force a reboot, or you can change critical settings accidentally.

It is also possible to get into the exciter using ftp, telnet, and ssh. You will need to consult your exciter's manual or manufacturer to set up and use these methods.

5.6.18 Software updates

Periodically, software updates become available for the HD Radio exciter. Your manufacturer will let you know when an update is available and what it does. Follow the directions that come with the update. Normally, you only need to reinput your VNC password, as the exciter configuration is saved on a flash drive. Some, like the upgrade to version 2.3.3 for the DexStar, required that the *Magnitude/Phase Delay* be reset, as the result of the upgrade was that the latency through the system changed. In general, most updates will completely rebuild the file structure of the exciter, in addition to updating the software. Follow the directions, reload your configuration from the flash drive, and you will be in good shape.

Note that updates are generally available via Internet download. The file you download is an .iso file. It is an image of the exciter's hard drive. You will need to have a CD burning program that can correctly burn an .iso file, as the machine will need to boot from this CD-ROM.

5.6.19 Listening tests and maintenance

Once you have set everything up, and the transmitter is stable, you will want to take a test drive if you have an HD Radio receiver in the car. You should have a good sounding HD Radio signal and, if you took the time to properly set up the system, you should have digital coverage out to just beyond the station's one millivolt per meter contour.

Maintenance of the HD Radio system is fairly basic. As with a transmitter, there are numerous "readings" that you should log periodically. I also perform a planned exciter reboot three times per year, with the thought that the exciter is a computer. Memory in computers sometimes, for no apparent reason, may become corrupted. Periodic reboots will generally prevent trouble from happening.

5.7 Moseley Starlink note

Some versions of the Moseley Starlink 950-MHz STL system did not properly set the "audio" bit in the AES-3 audio data stream. Additionally, the AES-3 protocol uses an "emphasis" bit. Older Moseley units not having the audio bit set and having the emphasis bit set could cause audio drop outs or complete muting of the AES-3 audio data from the studio.

Newer Moseley Starlink units do not exhibit this problem.

If you have an older Moseley Starlink unit, you may wish to contact Moseley regarding the fix for these issues. The fix is fairly simple to implement and involves either the setting of dip switches or the bridging of solder pads.

The Harris Premiere Web site has an easy field modification for the Moseley Starlink that will solve this issue. Log into the Harris Premiere Web site and perform a search for "Moseley".

5.8 PAD

Analog FM radio has, for a long time, had the ability to send certain PAD to listener's radio, such as title and artist of the song currently playing. This is accomplished through an RDS data subcarrier of 57 kHz injected along with the transmitted stereo baseband. The radio would interpret the data sent on the RDS 57-kHz subcarrier, and display title and artist information on the listener's radio (if it was RDS-equipped).

With the AM HD Radio system, AM stations for the first time have the ability to send title and artist information, along with several other fields, to listener's radio. It is a good idea for a station to utilize PAD. It will give radio manufacturers incentive to make sure this feature is included in future radio models, and it helps AM radio to be more competitive with FM and satellite radio because they also provide PAD.

The fields available for PAD are Title, Artist, Album, Genre, Comment, Commercial, and Reference Identifier. The PAD fields can be defined as such:

- *TITLE* – Song title or other program information.
- *ARTIST* – Song artist or other program information.

- *ALBUM* – Album the song can be found on or other program information.
- *GENRE* – Information about the type of program.
- *COMMENT* – A short description or comment on program content.
- *COMMERCIAL* – This can include various information, such as price and seller name, and can be used to transmit a picture.
- *REFERENCE IDENTIFIER* – An identifier used for the owner of the material.

PAD is derived from and defined in the ID3 tag specifications that are contained in the header of most music cuts on CD or on your automation system. More information on ID3 data can be found at http://www.id3.org.

It is most common to send the Title and Artist information fields. While this is obvious for music stations, talk stations could send title of the program and either the host's name or call-in number; sports stations could send the score of the game. There are numerous uses of Title and Artist data.

Many digital automation systems have add-on modules to send PAD into the HD Radio exciter. There are also stand-alone programs available that can send PAD information on a schedule.

PAD can reach the exciter for transmission in two ways. Most exciters will accept correctly formatted PAD on an available COM port. Data protocol is 1200 baud, no parity, 8 bits, 1 stop bit. The common method to send PAD to the exciter, however, is through TCP/IP connectivity.

PAD is sent to the exciter using TCP/IP port 10000. The exciter must have a static IP address and, if a firewall or Internet is involved, port 10000 must be opened to the exciter's IP address.

5.9 Exciter settings and what they do

The following settings and adjustments are found on the Harris DexStar HD Radio exciter. Software settings are found in irss version 2.3.3 of the iBiquity Digital Corporation HD Radio operating software. Some of these settings may be called something slightly different on exciters from other manufacturers, but all should be present and perform in the same manner.

MAGNITUDE LEVEL ADJUST – Adjusts the level of the magnitude signal sent to the transmitter's audio input. Usually located on the back of the exciter.

PHASE LEVEL ADJUST – Adjusts the level of the RF signal sent to the transmitter. Usually located on the back of the exciter or on the Digital UP Converter (DUC) card in the exciter.

BLEND CONTROL – Located on the *Audio Setup* screen. Sets a data flag that alerts the radio that it is OK to blend to the digital audio signal. Can be set to:

- *Blend* – Which tells the radio it is OK to blend from the analog audio to the digital audio.
- *Disable Blend* – The radio will not be allowed to blend to the digital audio, and the digital audio will not be accessible by the radio if the user attempts to force digital audio (may be indicated as "HD") on.
- *Disable, but allow selection* – The radio will not automatically blend to the digital audio, but the user can command the radio to do this.

DELAY ADJUSTMENT – Located on the *Audio Setup* screen. Sets the delay of the analog audio to match the delay of the digital audio to make a smooth blend.

RAMP CONTROL – Located on the *Audio Setup* screen. Allows the station to ramp into and out of time delay on the analog channel. Gives the station the ability to exit analog delay for programming such as live sporting events. In version 2.3.3 of the DexStar, the exciter is automatically set to disable blending during ramping or when the delay is fully out, but the listener can force his radio to the digital audio channel. Ramp in and Ramp out can be controlled by the station's remote control system.

RAMP RATE – Located on the *Audio Setup* screen. Determines how fast the exciter will ramp into or out of time delay. One sample is added or subtracted from the audio as per the number listed.

MODE CONTROL – Located on the *Mode Control* screen. Determines which HD Radio operational mode the exciter will operate in.

VNC PASSWORD – Located on the *Mode Control* screen. Allows you to change the password for VNC connectivity.

I/Q SCALE FACTOR – Located on the *Mode Control* screen. Sets the level of the composite Magnitude signal prior to the last digital-to-analog converter so that it does not overflow. The correct setting for AM operation is 12000.

DIGITAL CARRIER ON/OFF – Located on the *Mode Control* screen. Shuts off or turns on the HD Radio subcarriers. Can be controlled by the station's remote control system.

REMOTE CONTROL ON/OFF – Located on the *Mode Control* screen. Used to disable or enable remote control connections to the exciter.

MAGNITUDE/PHASE DELAY – Located on the *AM System Setup* screen. Used to time align the Magnitude and Phase signals through the transmitter. Can be set separately for day and night operation. Day/night selection can be controlled by the station's remote control system.

ANALOG GAIN – Located on the *AM System Setup* screen. Used to set internal AM carrier modulation of exciter with output of audio processor set to −3 dBFS.

MAG. CHANNEL DC OFFSET – Located on the *AM System Setup* screen. Used to null any DC offset voltage at the audio input to the transmitter.

PHASE Q SCALE FACTOR – Located on the *AM System Setup* screen. This should always be set to 1.

ANALOG AUDIO BW – Located on the *AM System Setup* screen. Sets the bandwidth mode of the exciter:

- *5 kHz* – Enables the exciter's internal 5-kHz brick-wall audio filter and tells the radio to operate in 5-kHz mode.
- *8 kHz* – Enables the exciter's internal 8-kHz brick-wall audio filter and tells the radio to operate in 8-kHz mode. Note that this audio filter is actually a 9-kHz filter as described in the NRSC-1-A standard. The original iBiquity Digital Corporation specification did include an 8-kHz filter.
- *BYPASS* – Disables the exciter's internal audio filtering, allowing 5-kHz audio filtering to be done in the audio processor. Tells the radio to operate in 5-kHz mode.

ANALOG MODULATION ON/OFF – Located on the *AM System Setup* screen. Used during setup to turn the analog channel modulation on or off.

LOWER/UPPER SB LEVEL – Located on the *AM System Setup* screen. Allows fine level setting of the primary HD Radio subcarriers as viewed on a spectrum analyzer. Primary subcarriers should be set to −28 dBc.

ENH. CARRIER PWR LEVEL – Located on the *AM System Setup* screen. When switched to *HIGH*, it will increase HD Radio carrier levels by 6 dB.

SIDEBAND INDICATOR – Located on the *AM System Setup* screen. No longer used.

CARRIER FREQUENCY – Located on the *Station ID* screen. Sets station carrier frequency.

COUNTRY CODE – Located on the *Station ID* screen. Identifies the country of origin of your station. Should be set to 1 for broadcasters in the United States. Other countries should refer to *ITU Operational Bulletin 763-1.V.2002* for information.

NETWORK ID – Located on the *Station ID* screen. Consult iBiquity Digital Corporation for this setting.

FACILITY ID – Located on the *Station ID* screen. Set to your FCC Facility ID.

LONG NAME – Located on the *Station ID* screen. The *Long Name* is displayed on some radios. Can be set to *Corporate* name, station slogan, or other wording.

CALL LETTERS – Located on the *Station ID* screen. Station call letters.

SONG ARTIST – Located on the *Station ID* screen. Part of the Internal PAD Generator of the exciter. Field should be blank to allow use of external PAD on listener's radio.

SONG TITLE – Located on the *Station ID* screen. Part of the Internal PAD Generator of the exciter. Field should be blank to allow use of external PAD on listener's radio.

GENRE – Located on the *Station ID* screen. Part of the Internal PAD Generator of the exciter. Field should be blank to allow use of external PAD on listener's radio.

ALBUM – Located on the *Station ID* screen. Part of the Internal PAD Generator of the exciter. Field should be blank to allow use of external PAD on listener's radio.

BIT ERROR RATE MODE – Located on the *Exciter Diagnostics* screen. Used to send a bit error detection pattern when used in conjunction with a test radio. Do not turn it on. The exciter will not send HD Radio digital audio when this is on.

SINGLE SUBCARRIER MODE – Located on the *Exciter Diagnostics* screen. Used to send only one HD Radio subcarrier at a time for testing purposes.

EXCITER TEST SCREEN – These buttons and functions are used for specific diagnostic purposes, and should only be used when troubleshooting with factory representatives.

HOSTNAME – Located on the *Network Configuration* screen. Allows setting of a host name, known as a computer name in Microsoft Windows. *Do not put a space in the host name*. The exciter may get stuck in a boot-up loop and need to be returned to the factory.

DOMAIN – Located on the *Network Configuration* screen. Used to set the domain name, if any, of the network to which the exciter will be attached.

IP ADDRESS – Located on the *Network Configuration* screen. Allows setting a static IP address for the exciter.

NET MASK – Located on the *Network Configuration* screen. Allows setting of the network mask for the exciter's network connection.

DEFAULT GATEWAY – Located on the *Network Configuration* screen. Allows setting of the Internet Gateway for IP Exciter access across the Internet.

NETWORK CONFIGURATION – Located on the *Network Configuration* screen.

- *Off Net* – Points the exciter to a default IP address and tells the exciter it is not connected to a computer network.

- *DHCP* – Allows the exciter's network IP address, *Net Mask*, and Gateway to be configured by the station's DHCP server.
- *Static IP* – Allows the exciter's IP address to be set.
- *Save Cfg.* – Saves network configuration. Exciter will need to reboot after configuration is changed.

GPS CONFIGURATION SCREEN – Shows GPS parameters and allows setting of certain parameters:

- *ANTENNA DELAY* (in nanoseconds) – This should be set as per a chart found in the exciter manual, and this is based on type and length of GPS antenna cable.
- *TIME ZONE* – Set for the time zone of your station.
- *DAYLIGHT SAVING TIME* – Check the box if your station's area observes *Daylight Saving Time*.

STATION SCHEDULER SCREEN – For future use, it will allow stations to dictate which parameters, such as call letters, time, and long station name, will be sent to radios in what order.

FAULT LOG – Will display any faults in the exciter. Note that the log will clear if the exciter reboots. The data is not saved.

EXCITER UPGRADE SCREEN – Allows saving of exciter configuration and upgrading of exciter software. Should be used with instructions from the manufacturer of the exciter for upgrading.

TOUCH SCREEN CALIBRATION – Everyone's eyes see slightly differently. This screen allows you to set where you think the center of a target is, and will make for easier touch screen operation.

Installing FM HD Radio and Making it Work

6

6.1 Getting started with the FM HD Radio installation

The FM version of the HD Radio system is very different from the AM version. In the AM version, parts of the HD Radio signal are buried under the audio and in quadrature with the carrier. In addition, the AM audio bandwidth is narrowed to 5 kHz to accommodate a set of HD Radio subcarriers in the region of 5–10 kHz from the unmodulated AM carrier.

The FM HD Radio system makes no demands on the analog FM signal. In fact, the FM HD Radio signal is a separate entity, operating at the far reaches of the FM channel. There is no need to narrow the bandwidth of the analog channel, FM stereo operation is not affected, and the station can still operate analog subcarriers, with the exception of operation of the HD Radio signal in extended partition mode in which a 92-kHz subcarrier will not work.

In hybrid FM HD Radio operation, the licensed analog transmitter power output (TPO) to the transmission line remains the same. The TPO of the digital transmitter as delivered to the transmission line is 1 percent of the analog power.

Generation of the FM HD Radio signal and the adjustments required to make the signal work has been greatly simplified by the introduction of the iBiquity-developed Exgine. With older methods, the present analog exciter worked along side the digital exciter to produce the hybrid waveform. The digital exciter was located at the transmitter site, usually along with the audio processing. As you can imagine, as many FM transmitter sites are located in remote areas, if the digital exciter or the processing system locked up, there was a great potential for the station to end up off the air.

With the development of the Exgine, several things changed. First, both the analog exciter and the digital exciter were replaced by one box: the Exgine exciter. The Exgine exciter generates both the analog FM signal *and* the digital signal, all in the same box. The audio processing can be moved to the studio location, making processing adjustments very convenient, and a new device called an Exporter is put in place at the studio to generate the HD Radio data for the Exgine exciter. This also opened the door for the analog audio to be routed through an external delay unit, sometimes as part of the audio processing, and to take a separate path to the transmitter site outside of the Exporter. If the Exporter were to crash, the analog signal is still present.

When you add an Importer to the system, a station now has the ability to partition the HD Radio data stream and add additional multicast channels to the operation. Both the analog audio data and the HD Radio digital data can be sent over a microwave STL or a T1 STL. We will be discussing the Exgine, Exporter, and Importer later in this chapter.

With the AM system, the entire HD Radio waveform is put through the AM transmitter and out to the antenna. There are several methods of transmitting FM HD Radio. This chapter will help you make sense of all of them, and make a decision as to what method to use to generate the HD Radio signal for your station.

Additionally, you will need the proper licensing agreement from iBiquity Digital Corporation to operate your main HD Radio channel. The license for the main HD Radio channel is a one-time payment. Contrary to what you may have heard, there is no "perpetual" fee to operate your main HD Radio channel. If you intend to operate multicast channels or sell utilization of your available data channels, iBiquity Digital Corporation does have a quarterly payment schedule for these additional services. Please consult with iBiquity Digital Corporation for specifics.

6.2 Internet access

While not completely vital to the operation of the HD Radio system, you should consider having Internet access installed at the transmitter facility. Whether it is a dedicated DSL line, or if you bring it in via microwave or through the T1 you are using to bring audio to the site is irrelevant. Having the largest "pipe" available coming into the site is not relevant, either. It is important that the Internet access is always on.

Later on, you will see where Internet access comes into play. Briefly, having Internet access at the site will allow you to get into the exciter remotely to assess a possible situation. I have been able to get into an exciter, spot an error in the process of starting, and reboot the exciter before it had a chance to crash and take the station off the air.

It should be noted, however, that IP access, either through microwave STL or T1 STL, is a requirement. The HD Radio data stream is delivered from the Exporter to the Exgine exciter through an IP connection. When planning your STL, please make sure to plan for an IP path of at least 300 kb bandwidth.

6.2.1 **IP connectivity**

IP connectivity to the transmitter site is important from three aspects. First, the HD Radio data stream is delivered to the Exgine exciter from the Exporter through an IP connection. Second, it will allow you to control the exciter, Exporter, and Importer from another location, such as your desk. Third, it is the preferred way to get PAD into the system.

IP connectivity can be through the Internet, over your bidirectional STL, through the use of a spread spectrum IP radio, or through dedicated T1 service. In the case of the HD Radio data stream from the Exporter to the exciter, however, you should avoid the Internet and use a more reliable IP connection, such as one provided through your STL system.

In parts of this chapter, you will see references made to IP ports. Each IP connection is divided into 65,535 separate data channels, called ports. It is these multiple ports that allow your computer to perform several tasks at once, for example, checking your e-mail while you surf the Internet.

Some specific ports are commonly assigned for certain duties. For example, connection to a Web site is typically through port 80. E-mail normally comes into your computer on port 110 and goes out on port 25. Depending on how your system is configured, you may need to open up certain ports to the outside world on your router. It is recommended that the Internet not be connected "naked" to your HD Radio equipment, but that it have, at a minimum, a router installed to protect the equipment from an Internet hacker.

If, for example, you will be bringing PAD into the system through an Internet connection, it would be wise to have a router on this connection as a point of defense against a hacker getting into your equipment. Because the router acts like a traffic cop stopping unauthorized entry, you will need to open up specific ports on the router so that outside traffic on these ports is allowed in.

If your company does not have an IT department, you should probably obtain a book such as "Networking for Dummies," which will explain these topics more fully. Knowing how to handle the IT aspects of the HD Radio equipment will make your job much easier.

6.3 **Environmental requirements**

Most transmitter facilities are "out of sight, out of mind" places. They are usually just adequate for the job of housing the station's transmitter and associated equipment. Many are poorly ventilated, and the ventilation is rarely filtered. Many building interiors are subject to temperature variations down to freezing in the winter and above 100°F in the summer.

The HD Radio exciter, Importer and Exporters are computers, as is the audio processor and the peripheral equipment. Consideration must be given to treating the equipment properly. This will help prevent lock-ups and help prevent the exciter from malfunctioning due to overheating.

This quote comes from the Harris DexStar manual:

> *Clean air is required. No salt air, polluted air, or sulfur air can be tolerated. A closed air system is recommended in these environments; that is, an air-conditioned room that recirculates, and properly filters the room air. No outside air is to be brought into the transmitter room.*

Obviously, they feel strongly about this topic.

It is strongly suggested that the transmitter building be air conditioned in the summer and heated in the winter. Keeping the room above 60°F in the winter and under 80°F in the summer will keep the HD Radio equipment operating correctly. Additionally, the equipment rack where the HD Radio equipment is housed should be equipped to move air through the rack.

Just as important as the temperature of the air in the room is that air be kept moving over heat-generating components. The idea is to constantly move the generated heat away from the components. In this way, even though heat is being generated, it can be managed.

If you will not be air conditioning the building, it is important to filter the outside air coming into the building. Dust and dirt on heat-generating surfaces acts like a blanket holding the heat in. It is also important to keep the air filters, if any, on the HD Radio equipment clean.

You will also need to make a decision regarding where to place your reject load. For stations running high power up the transmission line, the power in the reject load can be considerable and add considerable heat load to the transmitter room if it is kept indoors. Several manufacturers make loads that are intended for outdoor environments, and placing the reject load outdoors is recommended.

Because of the computers involved and the fact that your transmitter will be putting out higher power while transmitting an HD Radio signal, and putting excess power into a reject load, air conditioning is highly recommended, especially in warmer climates. If you are happy in the environment in the transmitter building, the HD Radio equipment will be happy. This will help to ensure that your HD Radio installation will operate well and remain stable.

FIGURE 6-1

Because of the heat that can be generated by the reject load, it is recommended that, if possible, it be placed outside the building in a secure location.

6.4 Methods of transmitting an FM HD Radio signal

There are several methods available to transmit an FM HD Radio signal. The method that you use depends on the power output of the transmitter and the overall efficiency you are willing to accept. There will also be considerations for redundancy.

To transmit the HD Radio signal, the amplifier used must be fairly linear – Class C amplifiers will not work. Tube transmitters will work with FM HD Radio systems, but the PA is generally biased Class AB. This brings the efficiency of the PA down dramatically from what we are used to seeing for tube PA efficiency. Rather than an efficiency upwards of 85 percent, the PA efficiency will be somewhere between 35 and 50 percent. In most cases, you will be replacing your present transmitter, or at the very least, putting in an HD Radio transmitter to operate with your present transmitter.

The methods of FM HD Radio transmission currently in use are:

- High-level combining,
- Mid-level (or split-level) combining,
- Low-level combining,
- Separate antenna combining, and
- Dual-input antenna combining.

6.4.1 High-level combining

High-level combining allows you to use your present analog transmitter to transmit the analog portion of the hybrid HD Radio signal, and combines the output of a digital-only HD Radio transmitter with this signal to produce the complete hybrid FM HD Radio signal. The principal pieces of equipment used to do high-level combining are:

- The present (or new) analog transmitter,
- The HD Radio-only transmitter,
- The combiner,
- A reject load, and
- A filter or circulator (if required).

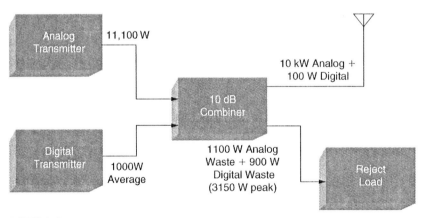

FIGURE 6-2

Block diagram of the high-level combined system.

Typically, the combiner used is a 10-dB combiner. With this combiner, 10 percent of the analog signal power is directed to the reject load. If the present analog transmitter is to be used (for the analog portion of the signal), it must have the overhead to make up for the 10 percent loss of power in order to deliver the licensed TPO to the transmission line. As an example, take a station operating with a TPO of 9.2 kW. The new output required from the transmitter to overcome the 10 percent power loss is:

$$\frac{\text{Licensed TPO}}{0.9} = \text{Required TPO} \qquad (6\text{-}1)$$

or approximately 11 percent more power is required to make up the difference.

In the above case:

$$\frac{9.2\,\text{kW}}{0.9} = 10.23\,\text{kW} \qquad (6\text{-}2)$$

The existing analog transmitter, in order to be used in a high-level combined system, must be able to produce 10.23 kW output power. In this case, 1.03 kW will be sent to the reject load as waste power in order to get 9.2 kW analog signal power out of the system.

The digital power for this station is one percent of the licensed TPO, so in this case it is 92 watts average. This next issue will be important when we discuss antennas for FM HD Radio transmission system. The average HD Radio TPO for this station is 92 watts. Because the HD Radio signal is extremely complex, the peak-to-average ratio (PAR) of the digital portion of the HD Radio signal is roughly 5.5 dB, or in other words, the peak digital signal power will be approximately 3.5 times the average digital signal power. For an average TPO of 92 watts, the peak TPO is

$$92\text{ watts} \times 3.5 = 322\text{ watts} \qquad (6\text{-}3)$$

or alternatively,

$$5.5\text{ dB} = 10\log\left(\frac{\text{Peak power}}{\text{Average power}}\right) \qquad (6\text{-}4)$$

Dividing both sides by 10:

$$0.55\text{ dB} = \log\left(\frac{\text{Peak power}}{\text{Average power}}\right) \qquad (6\text{-}5)$$

Taking the antilog of both sides:

$$10^{(0.55)} = \frac{\text{Peak power}}{\text{Average power}} \qquad (6\text{-}6)$$

$$3.548 = \frac{\text{Peak power}}{\text{Average power}} \qquad (6\text{-}7)$$

Multiplying both sides by average power to find peak power:

$$3.548 \times \text{Average power} = \text{Peak power} \qquad (6\text{-}8)$$

In the above example:

$$3.548 \times 0.92 \text{ watts} = 326.4 \text{ watts} \qquad (6\text{-}9)$$

Utilizing the 10-dB combiner, 10 percent of the analog signal power was directed to the reject load. Ninety percent of the digital signal power is directed to the reject load, while 10 percent makes its way to the antenna. Using the above example:

$$\text{Digital TPO} = \text{Digital power} \times 10 \qquad (6\text{-}10)$$

$$\text{Digital TPO} = 92 \text{ watts} \times 10 \qquad (6\text{-}11)$$

$$\text{Digital TPO} = 920 \text{ watts average} \qquad (6\text{-}12)$$

To get 92 watts average to the antenna, the HD Radio transmitter must produce 920 watts average power. Since 90 percent of the HD Radio transmitter's power is sent to the reject load, 828 watts average power is being sent to the reject load.

The HD Radio transmitter must be capable of producing the peak power of 3264.16 watts:

$$\text{Peak power} = 3.548 \times 920 \text{ watts} \qquad (6\text{-}13)$$

$$\text{Peak power} = 3264.16 \text{ watts} \qquad (6\text{-}14)$$

Therefore, using high-level combining:

- The analog signal transmitter must be capable of producing approximately 11 percent power above the present licensed TPO to deliver the licensed TPO to the transmission line at the output of the combiner.

- The HD Radio digital signal average power output is one percent of the licensed analog TPO. The digital signal transmitter must be capable of producing 35.48 times the average digital TPO power requirement (peak power) to produce the correct digital signal average TPO at the output of the combiner.

- The reject load used must be capable of handling, at the very least, the waste power from the analog transmitter plus the peak power of the digital transmitter.

- The transmission line must be able to handle the licensed analog TPO plus the resultant peak TPO of the digital transmitter. You may need to replace the transmission line to the antenna with the next size up.

- The antenna, after taking into consideration the efficiency of the transmission line, must be able to handle an input power greater or equal to the analog power delivered to the antenna plus the peak digital power

FIGURE 6-3

WFCR in Amherst, Massachusetts, uses high-level combining. Its analog transmitter is a Broadcast Electronics FM-20B running at 12.18 kW to achieve the licensed TPO of 11 kW. Its digital transmitter is a Harris Z6HD running at 1.1 kW to achieve 110 W digital TPO. Photo courtesy Charles Dube.

delivered to the antenna. You may find the need to replace the present antenna.

- Because the output required from the analog transmitter is higher to achieve the licensed TPO at the input to the transmission line, you will see the efficiency of the analog transmitter in its entirely is decreasing.

- Addition of the digital transmitter will see the total efficiency of transmitter operation decrease.

It may be necessary to install a filter or circulator at the output of the digital transmitter. This would be required if it is not possible to reduce the spectral regrowth and out-of-band products in the hybrid output (i.e., combined analog and digital) waveform. Depending on how much signal feeds through the combiner from one transmitter to the other, and depending on the characteristics of the amplifiers involved, the feed-through signal from one transmitter may be amplified by the other, usually the digital, transmitter. This would tend to produce out-of-band products. Installing a filter will minimize this.

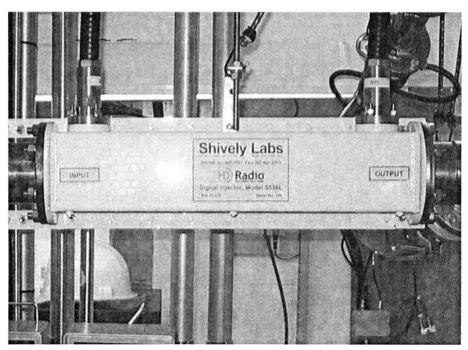

FIGURE 6-4

WFCR uses a Shively HD Radio injector as its high-level combiner. It is small in size and mounts easily near the ceiling. Photo courtesy Charles Dube.

High-level combining is usually used where the TPO is fairly high power, though the other methods can also be considered. With the advent of mid-level combined systems and high-power common amplification systems, high-level combining is becoming a less popular option.

Harris has a separate and combined common amplification online power calculator available at: http://www.broadcast.harris.com/radio/hdradio/calculator/default.asp, which will make your power calculations easier.

6.4.2 Mid-level (or split-level) combining

In mid-level combined systems, the analog signal is generated by two transmitters, while the digital signal is generated by only one of these two transmitters. There are several advantages to a mid-level system:

- The analog transmitter needs to produce less power output than licensed TPO rather than more power output as required in a high-level combined system. If your transmitter does not have the head-room to operate in a high-level system, you may be able to use it in a mid-level system.

- There is less waste power sent to the reject load.

- If your analog transmitter fails, the station will still have an analog signal on the air – granted, at reduced power, but the station will remain on the air.

Typically, the split-level system uses a 6-dB, 4.77-dB, or 3-dB combiner. This is determined by several factors, some of them are model of analog transmitter being used, analog power required, and the point where both transmitters would operate most efficiently.

Typically, the overall efficiency of a mid-level combined system is greater than that of a high-level combined system. Harris has a mid-level combined system online power calculator that can be found at: http://www.broadcast.harris.com/radio/hdradio/calculator2/index.html.

It is quite interesting to see what different combinations of combiners will do to the efficiency.

Therefore in mid-level combining:

- The present analog transmitter operates at a reduced power level.

- The new digital transmitter will produce not only the digital signal but also a portion of the analog signal, just enough to make up for the reduction in analog TPO.

- It is generally more efficient than high-level combined systems.

FIGURE 6-5

The mid-level system at KWAV in Monterey, California. The Harris Z-10 transmitter on the left runs at 7.1-kW output. The Harris Z8HD transmitter on the right runs at 2.2-kW analog FM output and 92-watt average digital HD Radio output.

- It provides a backup for the analog signal should the analog transmitter fail.

- It puts far less waste power into the reject load, necessitating a much smaller reject load and putting less of a load on air-conditioning. Note that the reject load should still be rated to handle the peak power sent to the reject load by the digital transmitter in addition to the analog power sent to the reject load.

- The transmission line must be able to handle the licensed analog TPO plus the resultant peak TPO of the digital signal.

- The antenna, after taking into consideration the efficiency of the transmission line, must be able to handle an input power greater than the analog power plus the peak digital power delivered to the antenna.

FIGURE 6-6

The Dielectric 4.77-dB combiner used in the KWAV mid-level system.

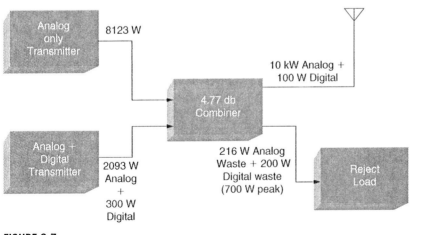

FIGURE 6-7

Block diagram of the mid-level (also called split level) combined system.

As with high-level combining, it may be necessary to install a filter or circulator at the output of the digital transmitter if you find that out-of-band products cannot be minimized. This is because the power from one of the transmitters that appears in the combiner at the output of the other transmitter may be amplified and sent back out through the system. Adding a filter will increase isolation and minimize out-of-band products.

6.4.3 Common amplification or low-level combining

In a common amplified system, the analog and digital signals are combined at a point before the PA. This method greatly simplifies things, as you are only dealing with one transmitter. It would be advisable, however, to have the old analog transmitter ready to go and plumbed into the system in the event of a failure of the analog plus digital transmitter.

Formerly, common amplification was only available up to a certain power level, as solid-state transmitters were not available for stations requiring high

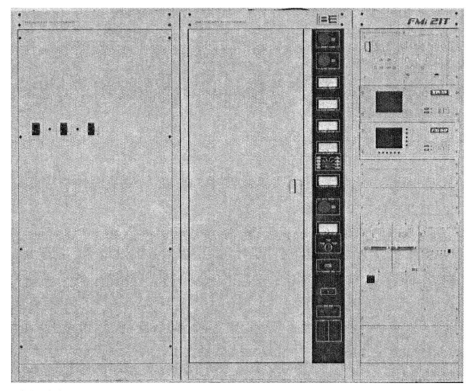

FIGURE 6-8

Broadcast Electronics' tube-type FM HD Radio transmitter. Common amplification simplifies transmitter installation. Photo credit courtesy of Broadcast Electronics.

power. In the past several years, however, Harris, Broadcast Electronics, and Continental Electronics have come out with tube-type FM HD Radio transmitters. All three manufacturers have tube-type common amplification transmitters that will operate up to 25-kW output. Continental Electronics will produce 30-kW output if you purchase the liquid-cooled version. As a general rule, solid-state common amplified transmitters are available up to about the 10-kW level. Check with your preferred manufacturer.

Tube-type digital transmitters generally operate at much lower efficiency than their Class C counterparts as they are generally operated Class AB. Because of this, they will also generate more heat than their Class C counterparts. Tube-type transmitters for HD Radio could be a good solution for stations requiring high TPO and desiring a simpler installation.

Therefore,:

- Common amplification simplifies things, as there is only one transmitter to produce the analog and digital signals.
- Transmitters are available in solid state and tube type for stations requiring high TPO.
- There is no reject load or combiner to be concerned with.
- Transmitters will output more heat than other FM transmitters. This should be kept in mind when planning air conditioning or airflow.
- The transmission line must be able to handle the licensed analog TPO plus the resultant peak TPO of the digital signal.
- The antenna, after taking into consideration the efficiency of the transmission line, must be able to handle an input power greater than the analog power plus the peak digital power delivered to the antenna.

6.4.4 Separate antenna combining or dual-feed antennas

It is possible to operate with the analog transmitter connected to one antenna and the digital transmitter connected to a different antenna. This will be discussed in Section 6.

6.5 Equipment required for FM HD Radio installations

Once you have decided on a method to get the HD Radio signal on the air, there is equipment that is common to FM HD Radio transmission. In the previous chapters, we discussed needing a separate audio processor and an STL that can handle not only AES-3 audio, but also an Ethernet connection. Microwave STL systems are generally one way, and the HD Radio equipment takes this into account by providing a mode for one-way Ethernet connectivity.

To put an FM station on the air, therefore, you need:

- An HD Radio transmitter using the combining method determined best for your station, including any changes required in the transmission line or antenna, and all additional equipment as called for by the combining method.

- The Exgine exciter.

- An HD Radio Exporter.

- An HD Radio Importer if you intend to operate multicast channels or broadcast advanced data services (beyond program service data).

- Audio processing for the main HD Radio channel (one processor for analog audio, one processor for digital audio).

- Audio processors, if you will be operating multicast channels, for each multicast channel.

- True average reading wattmeters, particularly important in a mid-level combined system.

- A spectrum analyzer for setup.

- A method to measure FM and HD Radio modulation, with the ability to split the analog and digital audio channels to facilitate adjustment of the analog time delay and level matching.

6.6 The FM antenna system

6.6.1 Single antenna operation

In most installations, hybrid FM HD Radio operation will utilize one antenna common to both the analog and digital signals, usually the existing antenna used by the station. The advantage of this, besides the simplicity of having only one antenna, is that the power ratio between the analog and the digital portions of the signal will be the same throughout the coverage area of the station (the analog signal will be 20 dB greater than the digital). This is a requirement in the FCC regulations. There are, however, conditions that must be met before the present antenna can be deemed capable of supporting HD Radio transmission:

- The bandwidth of the antenna must be at least 400-kHz wide, having a 1.2:1 maximum VSWR over this passband since the FM HD Radio hybrid signal is 400-kHz wide. Note that the majority of FM antennas should pass this test.

- The bandwidth of any multistation combiners or isocouplers in the system must be sufficient to pass the FM HD Radio hybrid signal.

- The antenna must be able to handle the analog power plus the peak power level of the digital portion of the HD Radio signal available at its input.

- The transmission line must be able to handle the analog power level plus the peak power level of the digital portion of the HD Radio signal at the transmitter or combiner output.

- Any isocouplers or combiners for multistation antennas must be able to handle the analog power plus the peak power level of the digital portion of the HD Radio signal available at its input, and must exhibit enough bandwidth to pass the HD Radio hybrid signal.

- Multistation combiners must provide sufficient isolation to prevent intermodulation products from forming and being present in the system.

Information on the power-handling capabilities of transmission lines is available from transmission line manufacturers. You should consult the manufacturer of the antenna, isocoupler, or multistation combiner for information pertaining to HD Radio operation.

6.6.2 Separate antennas

It is possible to operate with the analog transmitter feeding one antenna while the HD Radio digital transmitter feeds a second antenna. The FCC requires notification within 10 days of beginning operation with separate antennas. One advantage of using separate antennas would be that there are no combiners or combiner power losses to deal with.

To operate with separate antennas, a station must meet the following criteria as set forth by the FCC:

- The digital transmitter must use a licensed auxiliary antenna.
- The auxiliary antenna must be within three seconds of the latitude and longitude of the main antenna.
- The height above average terrain of the auxiliary antenna must be between 70 and 100 percent of the height above average terrain of the main antenna.

The digital portion of the HD Radio signal is required to be contained within the licensed contours of the analog signal. In other words, the separate antenna cannot give the digital signal a coverage advantage over the analog signal. Additionally, as a practical matter, there must be at least 40 dB of isolation between antennas to keep intermodulation products down. If this is not the case, sufficient filtering must be provided to prevent intermodulation products from forming.

Notification of separate antenna operation to the FCC must include:

- The geographic coordinates of the antennas.
- The elevation data of the antennas.
- The license file number of the auxiliary antenna to be used.

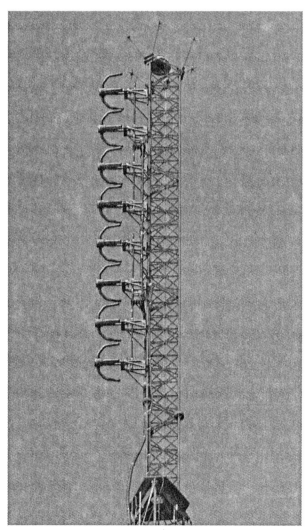

FIGURE 6-9

A dual-fed antenna. Photo credit courtesy of Electronics Research, Inc.

6.6.3 **Dual-fed antennas**

Some stations may wish not to combine the analog and the digital signals at the transmitter, but keep the feeds separate and let the antenna perform the combining. Several manufacturers have dual-fed antennas available that perform the signal combining in the antenna elements. Since the same antenna elements are used to transmit both the digital and analog signals, no special authorization from the FCC is required for operation.

In the dual-fed antenna, the combining of the signal takes place in the antenna elements. The dual-fed antenna incorporates the necessary hybrids to keep the analog and digital signals separate, yet allow combining to take place.

The dual-fed antenna requires two transmission lines to run up the tower. Typically, the digital transmission line is smaller, as the power from the digital transmitter is significantly less. That being said, you should have the tower analyzed before committing to a dual-fed antenna to ensure that the tower structure will be able to withstand the additional transmission line and combining component weights and wind loads.

6.6.4 **Interleaved antennas**

It is also possible to use an antenna configuration that incorporates separate bays for both the analog and digital signals – this is called "interleaved antennas." The analog and digital bays are usually interspersed among each other. Typically, the analog and the digital bays are polarized opposite from each other to help with isolation.

The advantages of using interleaved antennas is that the analog and digital signals are kept apart and actually feed separate antennas, and the digital signal is transmitted from the same aperture on the tower from which the analog signal is transmitted.

The disadvantage is that, as with the dual-fed antenna, a second transmission line is required to run up the tower. Additionally, circulators or filters may be required on the tower with the antennas. The tower would need to be able to handle the additional weight and wind load of the additional transmission line and any other components.

6.7 **Installing the HD Radio equipment**

First and foremost, each piece of HD Radio equipment is a computer. The Exgine exciter is a computer running the Linux operating system. Currently, the Exporter runs Microsoft Windows XP Professional, as does the Importer. While Linux is very stable and based on the UNIX operating system,

FIGURE 6-10

Interleaved antennas. Photo credit courtesy Bob Surette, Shively Labs.

there is a shutdown procedure Linux must go through, very much like Windows. It is strongly recommended that the Exgine exciter, the Importer, and the Exporter be connected to power through a UPS, and that the UPS be connected to the HD Radio equipment so that they talk to each other. Consequently, in case of a power failure, the HD Radio equipment should stay up and not crash. If there is no backup power available at the site, the computers should shut down gracefully. This should prevent corrupted files, and the possibility that the station may be off the air for several minutes when power returns and the computers reboot.

Next, a spectrum analyzer is required for FM HD Radio installation. The spectrum analyzer needs to be able to scan the entire FM broadcast band, and must be capable of a resolution bandwidth of 1 kHz or less. You should also have some type of HD Radio receiver available – one in which you can split the analog channel off to the left channel, and the digital channel off to the right channel so they can be heard together. It would be preferable to use something like the Day Sequerra M4 or M2 monitors, or the Audemat-Aztec Goldeneagle HD FM. The receiver is used to set the time delay between the digital and analog channels and to assist with balancing the audio levels between the digital and analog channels.

FIGURE 6-11

The reject load, an Altronic Research outdoor load, was mounted to concrete blocks behind the transmitter building at WFCR. Photo courtesy Charles Dube.

You also should decide where you will place the reject load if you are not using a common amplified, dual antenna, or interleaved antennas system. Depending on the power level and the combining method used, the power to be delivered to and to be converted to heat in the reject load can be significant and will heat up the room. If you have an indoor load, make sure you place it so that the heat it gives off will have no chance of igniting anything in the building. If you are using an outdoor load, make sure it will be stable (perhaps mounted on a concrete slab rather than just sitting on the ground) and is not placed where the heat given off can ignite anything.

6.7.1 Connecting the HD Radio Exgine exciter to the transmitter

There are a couple of ways that the Exgine exciter can be connected to the transmitter, depending on configuration.

If you are using common amplification, the RF output of the Exgine exciter connects to the transmitter's RF input. The control interface between the exciter and the transmitter should be connected so that the Exgine exciter brings its RF output on and off with the transmitter.

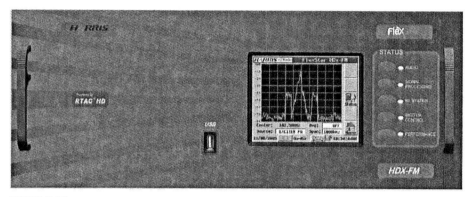

FIGURE 6-12

The Harris FlexStar™ Exgine exciter. Photo credit courtesy of Harris Corporation.

If you are using mid-level combining or high-level combining, you will need to make use of the two RF output connectors on the Exgine exciter. One is a normal RF output and, in this situation, is usually used to drive the analog-only transmitter. The other output is usually of a lower level, and connects to the digital-only transmitter in a high-level combined system or to the digital plus analog transmitter in a mid-level combined system. This output normally connects to a low-level amplifier in the digital transmitter. Control interface connections should be connected to both the analog and digital transmitters.

You will also find a connector on the back of the Exgine exciter to connect to a coupler in the digital transmitter. This is for the adaptive-correction system sample and needs to be connected (if adaptive correction is to be used). Follow the paperwork that came with your system from the manufacturer.

6.7.2 Giving the Exgine exciter inputs

If you will be feeding the Exgine exciter standard composite baseband audio for the analog channel, you will find a connector for this input. You will also find inputs for analog Subsidiary Communication Authorization subcarriers (SCAs) on the back of the Exgine exciter.

If you are using the recommended method of connecting an AES-3 signal for the analog audio, you should connect this to the main AES connector. Note that the Exgine exciter also provides inputs for analog left and right audio, as well as an input for SCA audio.

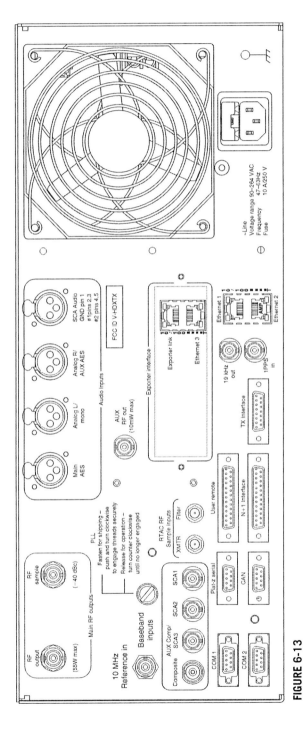

FIGURE 6-13

The rear of the FlexStar exciter showing the different connections. Photo credit courtesy Harris Corporation.

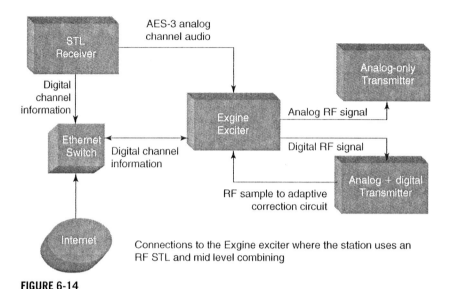

Connections to the Exgine exciter where the station uses an RF STL and mid level combining

FIGURE 6-14

Block diagram showing connections to the Exgine exciter in a mid level combined system.

When you connect the AES-3 connector, the Exgine exciter will be generating a composite stereo signal internally for the analog audio. We will discuss adjusting this later in this chapter. Note also that the Exgine exciter will offer a "hot backup" option for the analog audio, which allows you to choose, say, AES-3 as the primary analog audio input, and composite as a backup source. If the AES-3 signal were to go away, as in a failure of a digital STL, you could revert to an analog STL and get the station's analog signal back on using a composite signal.

The HD Radio digital signal will come into the Exgine exciter through Ethernet. This can be a connection directly from the Exporter if your Exporter is on site, but more commonly it will come from the STL. You will find an Ethernet connector for the Exporter on the Exgine exciter. Note that most exciters have more than one Ethernet jack on them. Refer to the manufacturer's instructions and make sure you connect to the proper jack.

6.7.3 **Where to install wattmeters**

Wattmeters are important to the correct operation of the HD Radio system. Older wattmeters cannot be used in an HD Radio installation. The waveform from the HD Radio digital transmitter is extremely complex, and normal wattmeters will read the output of the HD Radio digital transmitter incorrectly.

FIGURE 6-15

True average-reading wattmeters are required with an FM HD Radio system. Normal average-reading wattmeters will not produce an accurate reading due to the complexity of the FM HD Radio signal.

The newer style true average wattmeters not only read the output of the HD Radio transmitter correctly, but also provide new functionality for the transmitter facility. If you have Internet access at the transmitter site, you could connect your wattmeters to the Internet and be able to access them from offsite. This ability could provide you with a wealth of information before you determine that a trip to the transmitter site is necessary.

In a common amplified system, you would want to put one wattmeter into the output of the transmitter or coaxial switch feeding the antenna. In a mid-level combined or high-level combined system, you would ideally install four wattmeters, but you could get away with two. If you are using two wattmeters, one should be installed at the output of the combiner or at the output of the coaxial switch feeding the antenna. The other wattmeter should be installed in the line feeding the reject load. This will show you the total power output to the antenna, and the power to the reject load, which is important in determining if the system is properly adjusted.

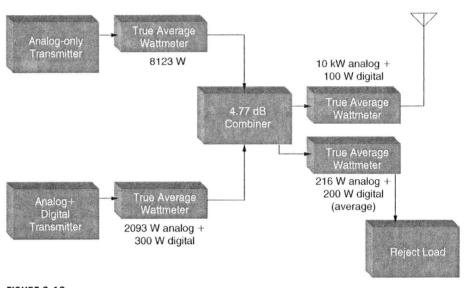

FIGURE 6-16

Diagram showing where wattmeters should be placed in a mid-level combined system.

If you have four wattmeters available, in addition to the placement described in the above paragraph, you should place one at the output of the analog transmitter and one at the output of the digital transmitter. This will give you additional measurements to see if the individual transmitters are operating correctly.

For separate or dual-fed antennas, one wattmeter would be installed in the line to the analog antenna input and one in the line to the digital antenna input.

6.7.4 Plugging in the Exporter

The Exporter can be placed either at the transmitter site or at the studio. If it is placed at the studio location, it will be easily accessible; the audio processor will also be at the studio and easily accessible. The Exporter is intended to be rack mounted.

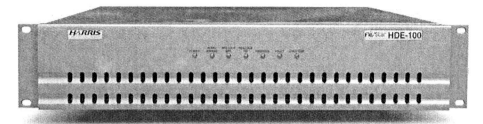

FIGURE 6-17

The Harris Exporter. Photo credit courtesy Harris Corporation.

The back of the Exporter has a jack for the analog audio AES-3 signal. If you wish to let the Exporter do the time delay, you should plug the analog AES-3 output from the analog processor in here. Keep in mind, though, that should the Exporter lockup, the analog transmitter will have no audio and the station will be off the air. If you intend to let the Exporter perform the time delay, the analog-out AES-3 signal from the Exporter should be connected to either the main AES-3 input on the Exgine exciter or to the AES-3 input on the STL.

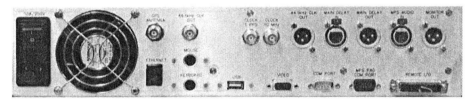

FIGURE 6-18

The back of the Exporter showing connections. Photo credit courtesy Harris Corporation.

If you are letting the analog audio processor or an external delay unit perform the time delay, you should not connect the analog AES-3 signal to the Exporter. Bypass the Exporter, and connect the AES-3 output from the audio processor (if it is performing the delay) or from the delay unit (if you are using an external delay unit) to the main AES-3 input on the Exgine exciter or to the AES-3 input on the STL.

The AES-3 output of the digital audio processor should be connected to the Main Program Service (MPS) audio input on the Exporter. The Ethernet connector on the Exporter should be connected to the correct Ethernet connector on the Exgine exciter or to the Ethernet connector on the STL. It is possible to use an Ethernet crossover cable to connect the Exporter directly to these devices, but I like to use standard Ethernet cables and

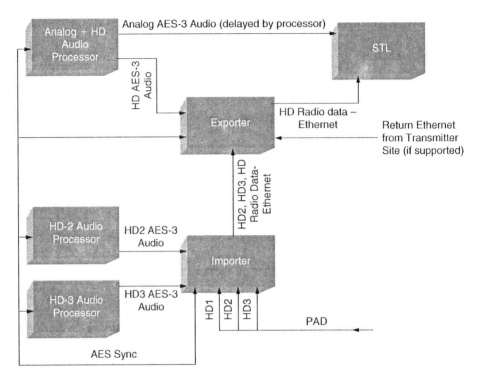

FM HD Radio Audio and data flow diagram

FIGURE 6-19

Block diagram showing audio flow from the processor to the Exporter for various modes of connection.

connect the Exporter and the Exciter to Ethernet 100-megabit switches. This will allow you to connect the Internet to the system, and to connect an Importer to add multicast channels.

If you use Ethernet switches, connect the Ethernet connector from the Exporter to one switch port. Then, connect the Ethernet connector from the STL to another switch port. At the transmitter site end, connect the Ethernet connector from the STL to one port on the Ethernet switch. Then, connect one port of the switch to the correct Ethernet connector on the Exgine exciter.

6.7.5 Connecting the GPS

The HD Radio Exporter comes with a GPS antenna. The GPS data provides the system with a real-time reference plus location information. The locking of Exporter GPS will also ensure carrier frequency stability, and help listeners' radios lock faster onto the various HD Radio stations in any given city. The GPS antenna needs to be mounted somewhere outside the building, perhaps on an STL antenna mount, and its coax cable connected to the Exporter.

The HD Radio Exporter is designed to work with GPS data. It is strongly suggested that you provide this connection since in some situations the Exporter may lock up without it. If you find that for some reason you cannot connect the GPS antenna, it is possible to tell the Exporter that it does not have a GPS antenna associated with it. However, it is best to have the GPS antenna connected and the GPS service activated in the Exporter.

It is interesting to note that you can use either 50-ohm or 75-ohm cable should you need to extend the length of the coax that comes with the

FIGURE 6-20

The supplied GPS antenna needs to be placed where it has a good view of the sky, such as on the station's STL tower.

exciter's GPS antenna. Just make sure to calculate the delay caused by the length of cable you use (this information is in the Exporter's manual), as you will enter this figure into the Exporter's configuration later.

6.7.6 Customer-supplied equipment

It should be noted that the Exporter and Importer do not come with a video monitor, mouse, or keyboard. These items will need to be supplied by the station and are required for setup and monitoring.

6.7.7 Powering up and configuring the Exporter

At this point, you can power up the Exporter. You will note that it boots into Microsoft Windows XP Professional. After Windows comes up, it will boot into the Exporter program.

When the Exporter boots to its GUI, you should notice that the metering under digital audio broadcasting (DAB) is showing audio levels. If you have the analog AES-3 connected to the Exporter, you should also see levels under the analog metering. If you do not have the analog AES-3 connected to the Exporter, the analog metering will show no levels, and this is normal.

You will also note that the screen shows that the GPS is unlocked. At this time, this is a normal condition. Since you have just powered up the

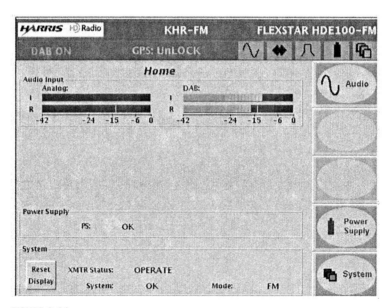

FIGURE 6-21

The Exporter screen shot. Photo credit courtesy Harris Corporation.

Exporter in a new location, it may take up to 15 minutes to lock on the GPS signal.

There are several items that need to be set up in the Exporter. My experience is with the Harris system. Since other manufacturers name some of their GUI screens and buttons differently, I will simply describe what you need to set. You will need to refer to your Exporter's instruction manual or simply click around to find these items.

6.7.8 System password

The first thing you should do is enter the system password so that you can configure the Exporter. Locate the password entry screen, and click on the password entry block. A virtual keyboard will pop up. Enter the default password (it is usually 1234 or 123456 depending on the manufacturer). At this time, you should change this password if the Exporter is in an area where it could be accessed by others. Make sure it is something you can easily remember.

6.7.9 GPS configuration

Next, locate the GPS Configuration screen. On the GPS screen, you need to pick your time zone, enter the antenna delay you calculated for the cable that is attached to the GPS antenna, select *Daylight Saving Time* if your location follows it, and select *GPS Time Sync* to set the time on the system.

6.7.10 Network configuration

The next screen you should locate is the Network Configuration screen. This screen may have already been set up by the manufacturer for your HD Radio system: if not, the manufacturer should have provided you with system IP addresses.

It may also ask you for a host name. I simply use the name *exp1* for Exporter 1. Note that this box cannot be blank, and should not contain spaces. If you accidentally put a space or other illegal character in this field, the Exporter may get stuck in a reboot loop and need to be returned to the manufacturer.

It may also ask you for a domain. It is OK to leave the domain set by the manufacturer in this field, or you can change it to another domain name of your choice. If the Exporter will be sitting on a network that uses a domain server, you should enter the correct domain name into this field.

The Network Configuration should be set for a static IP address. The reason for using static IP addressing in the system is so that IP addresses do not change – the exciter and Exporter know how to locate each other through their static IP addresses. Select an IP address for the exciter (or have your IT department assign it one) if the manufacturer has not yet assigned it an address. Set the net mask, which is typically 255.255.255.0. Set the default gateway (for Internet activity) to the correct IP address.

The Exciter MAC address should be set for the MAC address of the correct Ethernet port on your Exciter. A MAC address is a unique number assigned to each and every Ethernet device and is independent of the IP address assigned to this device. If you are using an Ethernet link over your microwave, you will only have one-way connectivity. Setting the Exciter MAC address tells the Exporter not to look for responses from the Exgine exciter. It also makes sure the UDP data packets are sent specifically to the Exgine exciter's MAC address. Not setting this address can result in lost timing packets, the diversity delay timing being off, and possibly the lockup of the Exporter.

The Exciter Link field also tells the Exporter where to find the Exciter. It should be set to the IP address of the Exciter.

6.7.11 Station ID information

You should next locate the Station ID Information screen. On this screen, you will see a place to enter the country code – the country code for the United States is 1. The *Network ID* is assigned by the manufacturer of the system. In the United States, the *Facility ID* should be set to the FCC Facility ID for your station. This information can be found by doing an FM query at http://www.fcc.gov/mb/audio/fmq.html.

Next, you should enter in a *Long Station Name*. This can be some way to identify your station, for example, the station's slogan. The entry for the *Long Station Name* at WOR is "Real Talk Radio." Note that some HD Radio receivers will display this field, so do not put anything off-color into this field as a joke. This field must be populated. Some manufacturers put the Exporter's serial number into this field. Please change this field. Do not transmit your Exporter's serial number.

Finally, you should enter in the *Station Call Letters*. If there is a check box to append the call letters, check "append FM."

6.7.12 Mode control settings

You will find a screen for setting the mode of the Exporter. The mode should be set to Exporter and FM MP1 if you are operating in the standard FM hybrid mode. If your station is operating utilizing extended partitions, the mode should be set as follows:

- MP2 – to add a single extended partition to the digital waveform. A single extended partition will add an additional 12.4 kbps of data capacity to the FM hybrid HD Radio signal.

- MP3 – to add two extended partitions to the digital waveform. Two extended partitions will add an additional 24.8 kbps of data capacity to the FM hybrid HD Radio signal.

- MP11 – to add all four of the extended partitions to the digital waveform. Utilizing all of the extended partitions will add an additional 49.6 kbps of data capacity to the FM hybrid HD Radio signal.

You should set the *Digital Carriers* to ON, and, if you intend to control any aspects of the Exporter through the station's remote control, *Remote Control* to ON – otherwise, leave this setting OFF.

Finally, if you will need to access the Exporter through the Internet, you should set a password for VNC. VNC will be discussed later. If there is a button to set the VNC password on your Mode Control screen, you should set it now. Make sure it is something you can easily remember.

6.7.13 **Audio settings**

The final settings we will make to the Exporter before saving the configuration are to the Audio Settings.

First, set the *Blend Control* to Auto. This will allow listeners' HD Radio receivers to blend to the HD Radio digital audio signal. If the *Blend Control* is off, the listeners' radios will stay in analog mode.

If you are performing the time delay external to the Exporter, you do not need to enter a delay figure into the delay box. If you are using the Exporter to perform the time delay, enter 7.45159 into the New Delay box. Set the Ramp Rate to 100.

If you are performing the time delay in the Exporter, press the Ramp Up button to ramp up the delay. If you are performing the time delay externally, you do not need to perform a delay ramp-up.

6.7.14 **Backing up system information**

Before going further, you should back up the information you just entered into the Exporter. To do this, locate the Upgrade screen on your Exporter. Place the flash drive that came with your Exporter into an available USB port. Press the *Save Cfg* button. The system will tell you to put the flash drive into a USB port. Since you have already done this, press OK.

The system will warn you that once you proceed, the system will reboot. The reason it does this is that normally, once you perform a configuration save, the system reboots to an upgrade CD and proceeds to upgrade the system. Since we are not upgrading and have no upgrade CD, only a reboot will occur. Press *OK*. The system will tell you that it has saved the configuration information; then it will ask you to press **OK** to reboot. Do so and let the system reboot.

Once the Exporter comes back up, we are ready to start adjustments at the transmitter site.

6.8 Exciter and HD Radio transmitter adjustments

Now that the Exporter has been powered up, configured, and connected to the STL, it is time to configure the Exciter and put the HD Radio signal on the air.

First, make sure that the AES-3 output of the STL is connected to the main AES-3 audio input on the Exciter. Next, make sure the Ethernet connector of the STL is connected to the Exporter Link jack on the Exciter through a network switch.

6.8.1 Setting the audio parameters

Locate the Input Setup page on your Exgine exciter and tell the Exciter about the primary analog channel audio source. Depending on the Exciter, this is a touch screen drop-down menu to select from.

If you are using a "hot backup" audio source, you will also need to tell the Exciter which source is your backup. If you are using a backup source, you will want to make sure the automatic switching is enabled, and set the time delay that the switching operation will wait once it has determined that the main audio source has failed. Make sure to set this period long enough so that soft passages in music or pauses will not cause a false switch. Manual intervention is usually required to put the primary audio source back on the air, meaning a trip to the transmitter site.

You will also find parameters to set the input levels on the Exciter. Typically, the AES-3 input levels are set to -2.8 dBFS. If you are using analog audio inputs, make sure to set their operating levels. If you are using composite, make sure to set the composite operating levels.

If you are using AES-3 or analog audio inputs, the Exciter will be generating the FM stereo signal. Make sure to set the preemphasis to 75 microseconds (US standard).

6.8.2 Exciter output parameters

The Exciter Output Parameters screen shows various settings for the behavior of the outputs of the Exciter. First and obvious is the carrier frequency setting. This should be set to the carrier frequency of your station.

The HD Radio subcarriers should be enabled so that the Exgine exciter produces an HD Radio signal, and the Exciter needs to be told it is being fed from an Exporter.

The Exciter also needs to be told what to output. There are two outputs on the Exciter. Depending on what the manufacturer has said will be the function of these outputs is how they should be set. As an example, if this were a common amplified system, the main output would be set to *FM +HD*. If this were a mid-level combined system, chances are the main output would feed the analog-only transmitter, so the main output would be set to *FM*, while the second output would be set to *FM +HD*.

The Exciter Output Parameters screen also allows you to set the output power of the main output. If you are feeding the Exciter into an existing transmitter as FM only, you will need to set the output of the Exciter to match the output of the former analog-only exciter.

You will also find *HD Radio injection-level* settings on the Exciter Output Parameters screen. Please consult the information provided by the equipment manufacturer for these values, as these parameters control the level of the HD Radio subcarriers.

6.8.3 Adaptive precorrection

There are a number of factors that will affect the performance and our-of-band emissions from an FM HD Radio transmission system. The Exgine exciter contains adaptive precorrection. This system monitors the output of the digital transmitter and automatically makes corrections to the Exciter's output to automatically minimize out-of-band emissions and spectral regrowth.

First and foremost, the transmitter must be properly adjusted for the adaptive precorrection to do its job. For solid-state transmitters, this is generally not a problem, as there are generally not many adjustments that can be made to the transmitter.

Tube transmitters, however, are another story. You will need to carefully follow the manufacturer's directions for tuning of a tube digital transmitter. This would include not only the normal tuning adjustments, but also items such as setting the screen voltage. The screen voltage in a tube HD Radio transmitter is not used to control output power as with an analog FM transmitter, and is a critical setting.

Once the transmitter is properly set up, the adaptive precorrection will minimize the spectral regrowth and the FM hybrid HD Radio signal will fit nicely under the FCC mask. Turn the adaptive precorrection on and watch the spectrum analyzer while it cleans up the output of the transmitter.

6.8.4 PLL Sync

A very important parameter to set is the *PLL Sync*. This will force the Exciter to lock to the timing sync signal from the Exporter, and is especially important in setups where the Exporter data is being delivered to the Exciter by a one-way Ethernet connection (UDP). If the Exporter and exciter clocks are not in sync, audio dropouts may develop, and worse, the diversity delay will drift, causing bad blend events in listeners' radios.

Locate and set the *PLL Sync* setting to Exporter. Once this is done, you can verify operation by locating the Signal Processing status page. You should see YES or OK to all of the following:

- Exporter Sync Active
- Exporter Sync Enabled
- Exporter Sync Lock

Note that it could potentially take up to two hours for the Exciter PLL to lock to the Exporter. If your system is not yet reporting that it is sync-locked to the Exporter, simply wait a while. While two hours may seem like an excessive period to wait for the exciter to sync-lock to the Exporter, the audio data packets of the digital portion of the HD Radio waveform take priority during transmission. It may take up to two hours for the exciter to receive enough of the sync packets being sent from the Exporter to determine that both items are synchronized.

Once the Exciter is sync-locked, it is unplugged for approximately 15–20 seconds, then plugged back in. This will force the Exciter to relock, and will ensure that the diversity delay will not drift. Note that, depending on the data packets being delivered, it may take up to two hours for the exciter to resync.

There is a new development in exciter and Exporter sync. Not all manufacturers have implemented this new function.

During the transmission of the HD Radio data packets, it is possible that a few will be dropped here and there. It is also possible that the data could "bunch up" and not be taken into the exciter fast enough. In this case, since the audio payload data takes a first priority, it is possible that some of the timing packets will not reach the exciter. The timing packets tell the exciter what audio payload packets it should be expecting to see next in line and what the previous packets were. Knowing what packets the exciter should see helps the exciter determine if any audio payload packets are missing from the sequence. Timing packets keep the exciter synchronized to the Exporter.

There is now a way to utilize a return IP path from the transmitter that would allow the exciter to request a retransmission of missing packets from the Exporter. This path is usually separate from the incoming UDP data packet path. A device known as the Moseley LanLink is a good device to provide this connectivity back to the Exporter.

If the exciter determines that it is missing either an audio payload packet or has not seen a timing packet arrive for a while, it will request a retransmission over the return path. This will greatly aid in preventing dropouts and the possibility of time delay drift. It has been determined that, on an average, a station can expect a complete momentary audio dropout once every 45 minutes if timing packets are missing on an ongoing basis. Consult the manufacturer of your exciter and Exporter on how to implement this retransmission feature.

6.9 Measuring and adjusting the FM HD Radio hybrid signal for compliance

Once the Exciter is set up and locked to the Exporter, put the HD Radio system on the air.

6.9.1 Adjusting analog modulation

Locate the Output Setup screen on the exciter and temporarily shut the HD Radio subcarriers off. Measure the modulation with an FM modulation monitor. You should see a stereo pilot of between 8 and 10 percent.

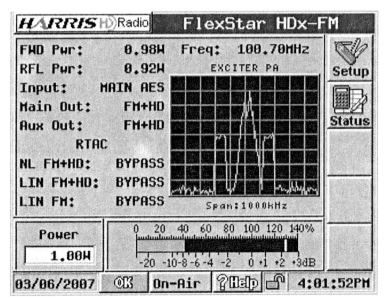

FIGURE 6-22

The normal monitor screen of the Harris FlexStar exciter. The spectrum analyzer display is for reference and is not valid for making compliance measurements. Photo credit courtesy Harris Corporation.

Total modulation should not be peaking above 100 percent (unless you are using FM subcarriers such as RDS). If the pilot level is off or if the total modulation is too high or too low, locate the adjustments on the Exgine exciter for pilot level and set the pilot to between 8 and 10 percent (I normally set it to 9 percent). Then, locate input level adjustments in the Audio Setup screen, and adjust the main input accordingly to attain 100 percent total modulation, though modulation should be correct if the output of the audio processor was set for $-2.8\,\mathrm{dBFS}$. Re-enable the HD Radio subcarriers.

6.9.2 Mid-level combined systems

Mid-level combined systems use one transmitter to output an analog-only signal, and a second transmitter to output a combined analog plus HD Radio signal. The first transmitter is run at a (significant) fraction of the required analog power. The second transmitter is run at a power level to make up the required analog power and also outputs the digital portion of the HD Radio signal.

Because you have the same RF signal sent to both transmitters, variations in cable lengths, in component tolerances, and in the RF path through the individual transmitters will mean that the signals are not perfectly in phase when they combine. If the signals are not in phase, the reject load power will be higher than calculated for best system efficiency.

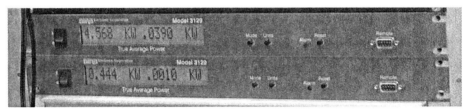

FIGURE 6-23

True averaging wattmeters assist with proper mid-level combined system setup.

To adjust the phasing of the transmitters, locate the *SLC* or *MLC Phase Adjustment* on the Output Setup screen. Start entering in phase correction adjustments, plus or minus, and set the power going to the reject load as per the manufacturer's instruction. You will also see the total output power increase slightly, but the reject load power is the one you need to pay attention to. Once you have set the reject load power, make sure to log this number for reference. If you notice that the reject load power is inching up, it may indicate a problem somewhere in the system. You can reset the reject load power by changing the MLC Phase Adjustment, and you will have the original phase adjustment for reference. If you notice that you have had to make a significant adjustment to the MLC Phase to keep the reject load power where it belongs, this may indicate a problem with part of the transmission system that needs to be investigated. Note that the reject load power will most likely be at minimum with the correct setting.

6.9.3 Tube-type HD Radio transmitters

Particular attention must be paid to the tuning and screen voltage adjustments of the tube-type FM HD Radio transmitter. It is important that the tuning networks be set to the center of their respective passbands. Having the tuning too far off center will create out-of-band products, and the system may not meet the spectral mask.

Power control of a tube-type HD Radio transmitter is done differently, and the screen voltage is not changed for power adjustment. Follow the manufacturer's directions closely for proper setting of the screen voltage as well as the proper method for tuning the final amplifier.

6.9.4 Setting up the spectrum analyzer

The spectrum analyzer input should preferably come from an output sample on the transmission line leading up to the antenna. If this is not available, an antenna feeding the spectrum analyzer would be acceptable.

First, make sure you have attenuators available to reduce the input level to the spectrum analyzer. This is important for two reasons: first, you do not want to blow out the input section of the analyzer and second, you do not want to overdrive the spectrum analyzer and create false indications of out-of-band emissions.

It is also recommended that, if your station is colocated with others, you have notch filters available tuned to each of the other frequencies at the site. These other strong signals may overload the front end of the spectrum analyzer, and notching them out is the best way to make sure they do not influence your measurements.

As a reminder, with analog FM, the power across an FM channel remains the same with modulation. There are many instances where the analog carrier will disappear, so carrier level on an FM station is constantly varying. This is as opposed to AM, where the carrier is at a constant level and power is added in the form of sidebands.

Preferably, you should set the analog carrier level on the spectrum analyzer with the carrier unmodulated. If you are performing these measurements during the day, chances are this would be inconvenient.

An acceptable method of setting unmodulated analog carrier level with modulation present is to reset the resolution bandwidth of the spectrum analyzer to a higher level, such as 1 MHz. Once the reference is established, the resolution bandwidth is reset for additional measurements.

To begin measurements while analog modulation is present, the spectrum analyzer should be set as follows:

- Center Frequency: carrier frequency
- Resolution Bandwidth: 1 MHz
- Span: 2 MHz
- Video Bandwidth: 1 kHz
- Sweep: leave in AUTO
- Average Type: video

Set the reference level on the analyzer with the top of the carrier just touching the top graticule. This will be your zero-dB reference. Add or subtract attenuators and adjust the analyzer's reference level to set the carrier level.

Now, reset the spectrum analyzer as follows:

- Center Frequency: carrier frequency
- Resolution Bandwidth: 1 kHz
- Span: 2 MHz
- Video Bandwidth: 1 kHz
- Sweep: leave in AUTO
- Average Type: video
- Average: ON, set to 100 averages
- If there is a sample point setting, set to the greatest number allowed, minimum 400.

After the average is done, you will want to observe the displayed spectrum. The FCC mask is defined as follows:

- Emissions from 0 to ± 120 kHz from carrier are referenced to 0 dBc.
- Emissions from 120 to 240 kHz must be attenuated to -25 dBc or greater.
- Emissions from 240 to 600 kHz must be attenuated to -35 dBc or greater.
- Emissions beyond 600 kHz must be attenuated to -80 dBc or $43 + 10 \log(10)$ (power in watts), whichever is less.

You should place a marker on anything that appears to exceed these limits and measure it, referenced to your carrier level setting at the top of the graticule.

Measure the level of the HD Radio subcarriers. They will be obvious at the outer reaches of the waveform, located from 129,361 to 198,402 Hz from carrier center frequency. The HD Radio waveform should be at a level of -45.8 dBc. If the HD Radio subcarriers are not at the correct level, you will need to go back to the Output Setup screen on the exciter and adjust the HD Radio injection level.

If you cannot bring the waveform into mask compliance, you should go back and recheck the settings on the digital transmitter and, if a tube

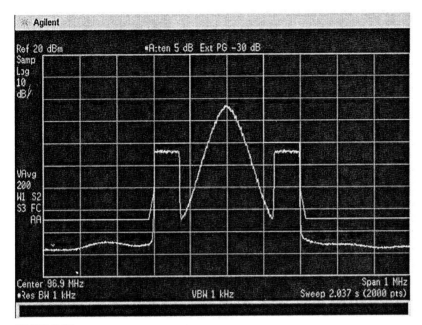

FIGURE 6-24

A correctly adjusted FM HD Radio system spectral shot.

transmitter, recheck the tuning. You may wish to go back to the adaptive precorrection screen and adjust the precorrector coefficients, adding or subtracting one, then disabling and re-enabling the adaptive precorrection to see if the waveform will fall into compliance.

If the waveform does not fall into compliance, the problem may be that you need to add a filter or circulator to the output of the digital transmitter. Chances are, though, that the adaptive precorrection will do its job and clean up the spectrum nicely.

You should save a screen shot at this point, then start checking above carrier for any spurious emissions. Check from carrier frequency to about 1 GHz. If there are other broadcast facilities close to your transmitter site, or if there are STL, Inter-City Relay links, or TSL transmitters located on site, make sure you know their frequencies and can document them on the spectrum analyzer display. Take screen shots. These will be included in your performance report to show emissions compliance.

6.10 Radio Data Systems

If you wish to run RDS data on the air, there are two ways to do so.

1. You can supply an RDS generator and input it to the exciter as an SCA. You will need to disable the internal RDS generator on the exciter to do so.

2. You can use the internal RDS generator on the exciter. You will find a setup screen for the RDS generator on the exciter GUI, where you can enter in the station call letters, slogan, and other information.

It should be noted that the RDS generator included in the exciter is not part of the iBiquity specification and has been placed there by the manufacturer. Some manufacturers have a method (called "scrolling PS") to utilize the RDS subcarrier for title and artist information. Others allow only the basic RDS information. Consult your manufacturer. You may be better off using an external RDS generator.

6.11 Multicast channels: enter the importer

In order to operate HD Radio multicast channels, an Importer is used. The Importer is a Microsoft Windows XP–based computer that works with the Exporter to partition the HD Radio data stream to allow the addition of extra channels. These are known as Supplemental Audio Services (SAS, the "multicast channels") or Advanced Application Services (AAS, the "advanced data" channels) to the Exporter.

6.11.1 Installing the Importer

The Importer should be located near the Exporter. The Importer should have its own static IP address. This address is entered through the typical Microsoft Windows Networking Connections screen. The Importer should have its Ethernet connection plugged into the networking switch for the system.

The audio input to the Importer is AES-3. The Importer will come supplied with a breakout cable that converts the D-connector on the Importer audio card to a standard XLR connector for AES-3 input.

6.11.2 AES-3 sync

All of the AES-3 connections to the Importer should be synchronized to the same clocking signal as the main channel audio. If you are using AES sync distribution at the studio location, you should make sure all of the audio processors are fed a sync signal. Failure to do so will cause audio dropouts, clicks, and pops in your multicast channels.

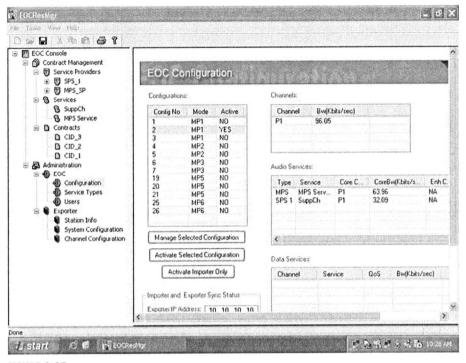

FIGURE 6-25

The Importer screen. The Importer is used to partition the HD Radio data stream and inserts the multicast channels and advanced data services. Photo courtesy of Harris Corporation.

If you do not have central AES sync distribution, you can get a sync signal from the Exporter. Use the 44.1-kHz out connection on the back of the Exporter to sync the multicast audio processor. If you are running more than one multicast channel, you will need either an AES distribution amplifier or an AES splitter. The AES signal relies on proper impedance and termination to operate properly. Please do not simply "Y" the sync output to several devices. You will be asking for trouble. AES distribution amplifiers and AES splitters are readily available devices.

It is recommended with newer Importers that the Importer audio card be directly clocked. In this case, I would also clock the audio processors as well.

6.11.3 Licensing of the Importer

There are two software licenses to be concerned with involving the Importer. The first is the Microsoft Windows license. Microsoft Windows was installed at the factory when the Importer was constructed and initially configured. Windows needs to be activated by your station within

30 days of factory configuration. If this is not done, you may find yourself locked out of the Windows operating system, and you will need to consult with either the manufacturer of the Importer or Microsoft. This activation is usually done over the Internet. If you do not have Internet connectivity to the Importer, it is possible to activate the product by telephone with a Microsoft representative.

The second license is the iBiquity Importer license key. When first started, the licensing manager will display a window with two fields and buttons. Both fields will be empty. Click on the button that says "Get Request Key," and the first window will populate. Write this number down, then e-mail it to iBiquity at importerkey@iBiquity.com. iBiquity will e-mail you back a 16 character activation key. Enter this key into the "License Key" window, and press the "Activate" button. Note that you will need to renew this license on a yearly basis. The Licensing Manager window will display the expiration date for the license that you have at present.

6.11.4 Importer configuration

The Importer works in conjunction with the Exporter to partition the available bandwidth of the HD Radio data stream. This will allow you to put additional multicast channels and advanced data services on the air.

The available data rate for the hybrid FM HD Radio signal is 96 kbps. You will need to decide how much of this data rate you wish to allocate to each multicast channel. Note that the lowest data rate that can be assigned to the main HD Radio channel is 32 kbps. The software will not allow you to set the data rate for the main digital channel any lower. This is the lowest data rate that will produce an HD Radio channel that meets the FCC's requirement: "Radio stations must provide a free digital audio programming service that is comparable to or better in audio quality than that of their current analog service."

It is assumed that the word "quality" in the FCC's requirement refers to the technical specifications for an analog FM signal: audio bandwidth being 50 Hz to 15 kHz. This is not normally obtainable with a data rate below 32 kbps. This is why the lowest data rate that can be set for the main HD Radio channel has been limited in software by iBiquity.

The higher the data rate for the main HD Radio channel, the better will be the quality. For example, you could allocate 64 kbps to the main channel, and 32 kbps to an HD-2 channel. There are at least eight different combinations available at the moment. You will need to work with the manufacturer to determine which setting is best for your needs.

You may also wish to turn on the extended partitions on your HD Radio signal by using what is called the "extended hybrid" mode of operation. This will allow you to maintain higher data rates on all of your HD Radio

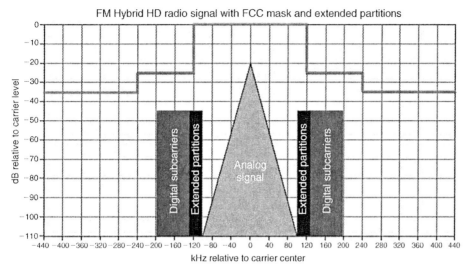

FIGURE 6-26

The FM HD Radio data stream partitioned for multicast channels.

channels by utilizing the additional data rate available with extended partitions. These extended partitions will be closer to the analog FM signal than are the normal digital subcarriers, so be sure to listen to make sure that these don't impact the audio quality of the analog signal.

Once you have determined how to partition your HD Radio signal, you will need to save the information and synchronize the Exporter. Doing so will change the data rate on the Exporter for the main channel. Unfortunately, the settings on the Importer are not straightforward. It is best to utilize the presets and consult with the manufacturer to determine your configuration settings.

The audio is input to the Importer in AES-3 fashion through XLR connectors. These audio channels appear on a virtual mixer, similar to the Windows audio mixer. You have the ability to adjust levels and data parameters for each audio channel.

6.12 **Firewall configuration**

If your Exporter, Importer, and exciter will be sitting behind a firewall, you will need to open the following ports for various forms of communications:

- Port 8145 to the exciter. This is the port used by the UDP connection between the Exporter and the exciter.

- Port 10000 through 10002 to the Exporter. This is the port used for PAD for the main HD Radio program channel.
- Port 4442 to the Importer. This is the port used for PAD for the HD1 channel.
- Port 4444 to the Importer. This is the port used for PAD for the HD2 channel.
- Port 4446 to the Importer. This is the port used for PAD for the HD3 channel.
- Port 9025 to the Exporter. This port is used for communication between the Importer and Exporter.
- Port 8025 to the Exporter. This port is used for communication between the Importer and Exporter.

6.13 **PAD**

PAD on the FM system is handled a bit differently than with the AM system. PAD is also referred to as Program Service Data or PSD. The FM system can transmit more channels, and that is one difference. The FM

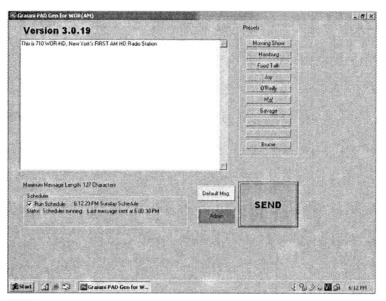

FIGURE 6-27

Screen shot of the PAD generation program used by WOR, New York. This particular program was written by a student member of the Society of Broadcast Engineers, Chapter 15.

system also uses an Exporter or can use just an exciter, which is another difference.

In general, you should obtain a program from either your automation company or another vendor to handle PAD. Depending on the software, you may need a version for each HD Radio channel that your station operates.

If your station is operating with just an exciter or Exporter, the PAD enters the system on port 10000. If you are using an Importer, the HD1-channel PAD enters on port 4442. The HD2-channel PAD enters on port 4444. The HD3-channel PAD enters on port 4446.

The fields available for PAD are: Title, Artist, Album, Genre, Comment, Commercial, and Reference Identifier. The PAD fields can be defined as such:

- *TITLE* – Song title or other program information.
- *ARTIST* – Song artist or other program information.
- *ALBUM* – Album the song can be found on or other program information.
- *GENRE* – Information about the type of program.
- *COMMENT* – A short description or comment on program content.
- *COMMERCIAL* – This can include numerous information such as price and seller name, and can be used to transmit a picture.
- *REFERENCE IDENTIFIER* – An identifier used for the owner of the material.

PAD is derived from and defined in the ID3 tag specifications that are contained in the header of most music cuts on CD or on your automation system. More information on ID3 data can be found at http://www.id3.org.

It is most common to send Title and Artist information. While this is obvious for music stations, talk stations could send title of the program and either the host's name or call in number; sports stations could send the score of the game. There are numerous uses of Title and Artist data.

6.14 **System maintenance**

Maintenance of the FM HD Radio transmission system is not much different than normal FM system maintenance. Care should be given to logging the reject load power periodically as well as looking at the transmitted spectrum to ensure the HD Radio signal is operating within the FCC mask.

While the Exporter, Importer, and Exgine exciter are, as a rule, stable, it would be a good idea to schedule periodic reboots of these devices just to be safe. Stations with HD Radio tube transmitters should check the spectrum if any tuning changes are made to the transmitter for any reason. According to Geoff Mendenhall at Harris, screen voltage in an HD Radio tube transmitter is probably one of the most critical parameters and can easily cause the transmitted signal not to meet the mask.

6.15 **Moseley Starlink Note**

Some versions of the Moseley Starlink 950-MHz STL system did not properly set the "audio" bit in the AES-3 audio data stream. Additionally, the AES-3 protocol uses an "emphasis" bit. Older Moseley units not having the audio bit set and having the emphasis bit set could cause audio drop outs or complete muting of the AES-3 audio data from the studio. Newer Moseley Starlink units do not exhibit this problem. If you have an older Moseley Starlink unit, you may wish to contact Moseley regarding the fix for these issues. The fix is fairly simple to implement and involves either the setting of dip switches or the bridging of solder pads.

The Harris Premiere Web site has an easy field modification for the Moseley Starlink that will solve this issue. Log into the Harris Premiere Web site, and perform a search for "Moseley".

6.16 **FM Conclusion**

As opposed to the AM HD Radio system, the FM HD Radio system has many different methods to get a signal on the air. The method that is right for your station is determined by many different factors.

While the equipment used in the AM HD Radio system is slightly different depending on each manufacturer, the equipment used in the FM HD Radio system is very different from one manufacturer to another. There is very little, in general, to adjust on the FM HD Radio system, so I will not spell out all the adjustments at the end of this chapter as I did with the AM system – particularly the adjustments in the Exgine exciter. Some of the adjustments are called something very different and it would be difficult to cross-index them here. In the several FM systems I have set up, though, these adjustments have been far easier to make and get up on the air than their AM counterparts. I'm sure you will find this the same.

Real-life Experiences
with HD Radio

The first part of this book deals with helping you get your HD Radio signal on the air. Hopefully, it has helped ease some of the confusion you may have been feeling and, if you are putting an FM HD Radio station on the air, has helped you sort out the various methods of combining the analog and digital signals.

The first part of this book is intended as an educational aid, and presents the information in factual form.

This part of the book discusses my personal experiences with operating a hybrid AM HD Radio station since October 2002. I have many observations to share with you with the hopes that you can get an idea of what to expect with the signal you put on the air. I also have experience with the FM HD Radio system, though not as much as with the AM system, so my observations will lean toward the AM HD Radio system.

I will tell you that being a pioneer with a new technology is not an easy job. Since signing WOR in New York on as New York's first AM HD Radio station on October 11, 2002, I have been:

- Called just about every name in the book, including some combinations I didn't think possible.

- Called "iBiquity's mouthpiece".

- Threatened, not only with physical violence but also with being taken in front of the Federal Communications Commission (FCC), to "be exposed for what I am".

- Harassed and stalked.

- Accused of being highly paid by iBiquity for my views on HD Radio and on my willingness to experiment and report my findings.

- Called "the killer of AM Radio".

- Accused of "starting this mess" and was told that I had "better fix it".   155

My parents being married at the time of my birth has been questioned.
My technical abilities and knowledge have been questioned.

All of this has been uncalled for. Moreover, all of this has been done by a relatively small group of people who, in my opinion, wish to continue living in the dark ages. If you have been in the business for any length of time, you know very well that our industry has been struggling for a while, as new technologies and gizmos have been luring the audience away from radio.

My basic belief is that radio needs to do something and come into modern times to survive. The first obvious area that comes to mind is programming, particularly with the advent of the iPod and satellite radio. I'm not a programmer and don't play one on television, but it doesn't take a rocket scientist to figure out that if someone can essentially program their own "radio station" with their own music collection on their iPod, or if they can hear music or other programs on satellite or Internet radio, they won't listen to us.

That being said, if a potential listener has the choice of listening to essentially the same program on a digital source or analog radio, I highly doubt the choice will be analog radio. In order for radio to remain competitive, it needs to evolve to digital.

It could have been relatively easy, had the FCC made additional spectrum available for a digital radio band then gradually easing out analog stations. This, in its basic form, is what the FCC did for HDTV – it assigned unused frequencies, essentially wasted spectrum, to digital television stations and set a sunset date for the analog stations.

Because the FCC did not make additional spectrum available for digital radio, it became necessary to adopt a hybrid analog/digital system, in-band on-channel (IBOC), or HD Radio. As with any hybrid system, there are compromises that must be made for both the digital and analog signals to coexist. Part of this is potential interference to adjacent channels in both the AM and FM bands. It requires a different way of thinking about AM and FM station coverage to ease the transition to digital. Incidentally, if you read the FCC's Report and Order authorizing the IBOC rules carefully, it is quite obvious that the FCC is looking toward a digital future for radio. Some think HD Radio is a fad and will soon go away. It will be with us for a long time based on statements made by the Commission.

So, in the spirit of full disclosure, I would like to address the previous bullet points:

- My vocabulary of foul language was becoming quite repetitive and boring before I became an HD Radio pioneer. Thanks to all who brought different combinations of words to my attention, thus broadening my horizons.

- I have never been a mouthpiece for anyone, and my statements and observations are strictly my own.

- Threats don't faze me; I have nothing to be concerned with regarding the FCC and, in fact, the FCC has quoted me in its proceedings; and I have nothing to hide – I am a broadcast engineer who stays current with the technology.

- Those who have harassed and stalked me have police folders with their names on them. I don't mess around.

- I have never been paid even a dime by iBiquity Digital Corporation (hereafter iBiquity). The only thing I have received from iBiquity, besides knowledge, a hearty pat on the back and a huge "thank you," is one of the first HD Radios when they became available – so I could listen to my station. Incidentally, WOR is held up as the gold standard of AM HD Radio digital audio, something I am extremely proud of.

- I have not killed AM radio. AM radio has been dying a slow death on its own over the years. If anything I did, I have helped slow or stop its death by putting an AM HD Radio signal on the air.

- I did not "start the mess." and have no intention of "fixing" what some perceive as problems with the hybrid HD Radio systems. I was one of the first to state that the HD Radio systems are not perfect. My job is to make the HD Radio systems we have perform to the best of their abilities. If I were not doing my job, I would not have been selected to write this book.

My technical abilities and knowledge are a matter of record with the FCC, The Society of Broadcast Engineers, the National Association of Broadcasters, the New Jersey Broadcasters Association, the New York Broadcasters Association, the Connecticut Broadcasters Association, and many broadcast engineers around the United States. I do not have to defend them.

Oh! And my parents were married almost three years when I was born.

I can also say that I have told the truth and will continue to tell the truth in regards to my HD Radio experiences, with my experiences being both good and bad. Some people may not like hearing the truth, and that is simply too bad. I will not bend my observations just because someone doesn't like what I have to say. While we may not always agree, it doesn't mean I will lead you astray. My opinion is my opinion and I am entitled to it, just as you are to yours. I back my opinion with not only 5 years of operating a hybrid AM HD Radio station under my belt, but also 30+ years of broadcast engineering.

Now that my introduction is out of the way, I will present several different stories to you, which will take you through my adventures with the HD Radio technology. It has been a fun, entertaining, and interesting learning experience. If you are reading this book, most likely you are either contemplating the conversion of a facility to HD Radio or have been told to make it happen. Regardless, I hope you find not only the first part of this book helpful, but also the following stories.

A.1 The beginning

In the spring of 2002, I was approached by iBiquityDigital Corporation. It was looking for a high-power AM broadcast facility in a large city for experimentation, the idea was to see how the hybrid AM HD Radio signal would propagate and survive in a "concrete canyon." New York City (NYC) was the perfect testing ground, with not only many canyons of concrete,

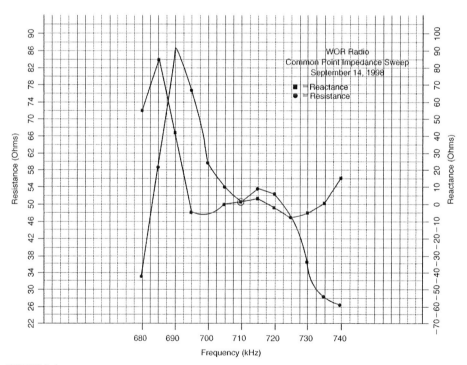

FIGURE A-1

The common point graph from the former WOR, Lyndhurst, New Jersey, transmitter facility. It was far from perfect, yet passed the HD Radio signal with no problem whatsoever.

but also electrical noise galore. iBiquity was also looking for a facility that wasn't necessarily perfect. WOR fits the bill nicely, as the Common Point graph of figure A-1 shows.

A discussion ensued with Rick Buckley, President of Buckley Broadcasting Corporation, WOR's parent, and Bob Bruno, Vice President/General Manager of WOR Radio. Would Buckley be interested in, essentially, lending WOR to iBiquity for the good of the industry? We had numerous questions for iBiquity, the first and foremost being what would happen if, in our determination, the WOR signal were damaged by the HD Radio signal.

iBiquity stated that, if we determine that WOR is suffering because of the HD Radio testing, we have the right to shut off the HD Radio signal and disconnect the equipment from the WOR main transmitter with little, if any, advance notice. With that question answered to our satisfaction, WOR embarked on being a pioneer in the next phase of broadcast technology for radio.

FIGURE A-2

This is the original HD Radio exciter installed at WOR by iBiquity Digital Corporation in 2002.

WOR, with the help of engineers from iBiquity, installed an iBiquity test exciter (figure A-2) on WOR's main transmitter, at that time a Harris DX-50. The exciter itself was a computer running the Linux operating system (which is like present-day exciters), with a ½ Video Graphics Array (VGA) touch screen installed into the front of the computer case.

FIGURE A-3

The EASU, the companion to the HD Radio exciter and its interface to the outside world.

With the exciter was an EASU (figure A-3), the Exciter Auxiliary Services Unit. This unit interfaced the exciter to the equipment installed in the Harris DX-50, and would force the system to switch to standard monaural analog modulation and the transmitter's internal oscillator in the event of a failure of the exciter.

Sitting on top of the Harris DX-50 transmitter was a small, gray box that was the interface between the iBiquity exciter and the transmitter (figure A-4). Both the RF and audio (or magnitude) signals from the exciter were sent to the transmitter through shielded Category-6 computer networking cable.

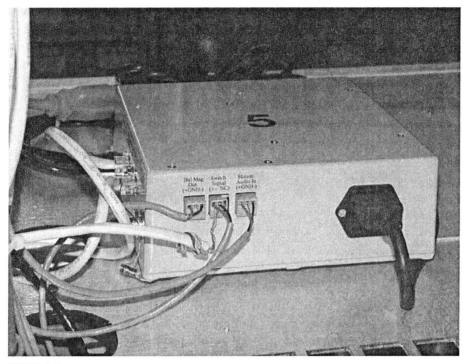

FIGURE A-4

The interface box sat on top of the Harris DX-50 transmitter. This box converted the phase signal from the exciter to a standard RF signal to drive the transmitter, and switched between the magnitude signal from the exciter and standard analog audio to feed the transmitter in the event of exciter failure. It also controlled a relay in the transmitter that would switch between the transmitter's internal oscillator and the RF from the exciter.

The interface box did several things. First, it converted the RF signal sent from the exciter to an unbalanced BNC connection to plug into the external oscillator port on the transmitter.

Next, it converted the magnitude signal from the exciter to balanced audio, which would connect to the transmitter's audio input.

The box also took the standard analog audio from the audio processor and put it through a relay. If the exciter failed, the relay would open putting the normal audio into the transmitter's audio input.

The last thing the box did was control a relay that was placed in the transmitter (figure A-5). This relay was switched between the internal oscillator in the transmitter and the RF signal supplied by the exciter. If the exciter failed, the box would switch the audio input to the transmitter back to the normal source, the output of the audio processor. It would

FIGURE A-5

This relay mounted in the DX-50 switched between the internal oscillator in the transmitter and the HD Radio exciter. It was controlled by the interface box sitting on top of the transmitter.

also switch the RF input of the transmitter back to its internal oscillator in the event of exciter failure. In this way, the station would remain on the air in mono mode should the exciter fail.

The transmitter tuned up nicely into the dummy load at 10,000 watts. We tried the transmitter at 50,000 watts and it ran just fine. We then put the transmitter on the air at 10,000 watts and fine-tuned the spectral regrowth. Finally, we put the transmitter on the air at 50,000 watts. It was happy for, oh, about five minutes when the transmitter started to glitch. It was acting as if it were seeing problems with the antenna, and muting its RF output momentarily in an attempt to correct the problem.

This is where I first learned that the output monitor circuitry in the transmitter could be too sensitive with the HD Radio signal present. While the transmitter was not being overmodulated in the negative direction, the HD Radio subcarriers add significant power to the sidebands of the transmitter that a normally adjusted output monitor would not expect to see.

FIGURE A-6

The rear of the iBiquity test exciter. Note the RJ-45 plugs connecting Cat-6 cable to the interface box on top of the transmitter.

The output monitor was acting as if it were seeing a "zero crossing," and muting the transmitter to protect itself.

Zero crossing. What the heck is that? If you observe the output of an AM transmitter on an oscilloscope, you will be observing it in a time domain. As you watch the RF envelope, you will see the RF carrier, and will normally set the level of this carrier on the screen as your reference. When modulation is applied, you see the amplitude of this waveform increases and decreases: an increase of the 2X unmodulated carrier voltage is 100 percent positive modulation, the carrier being pinched off at zero volts is 100 percent negative modulation.

If you are using a tone to modulate the carrier and then increase the level of that tone, you will overmodulate the transmitter in the negative direction. This causes two things to happen. First, the audio signal will clip in the negative direction as, in the time domain, you cannot have more than 100 percent negative modulation. Second, this clipping will cause spurious RF signals, or splatter, to be generated by the transmitter.

FIGURE A-7

Before a procedure was approved by Harris to desensitize the output monitor of the DX-50 transmitter, a temporary measure was approved. It involved grounding one of the fault inputs on the output monitor board to prevent false zero crossing trips.

With complex audio, you will observe something interesting on the scope. You will see what appears to be the negative peak crossing over the zero line. This is called a zero crossing. Most modern AM transmitters, if they detect a zero crossing (or, for that matter, a pinched off carrier), will briefly kill the output amplifier's output for protection. Metal Oxide Semiconductor Field Effect Transistor (MOSFET) amplifiers do not like to be underdriven, as this will destroy the transistors. A zero crossing appears to the transmitter that it has lost RF drive, and it will react in self-defense.

In the frequency domain, on a spectrum analyzer, you know that the AM carrier does not go away. But the effects of negative overmodulation can be seen as spurious emissions of intermodulation products produced by the transmitter. This is not a desirable condition and is, in fact, illegal to operate this way.

The brief (we're talking milliseconds) carrier clip off will cause pops in the demodulated analog audio. Because the carrier is literally going away when the transmitter protects itself, an HD Radio receiver will lose its reference and will not be able to lock onto the HD Radio subcarriers. It, therefore, will not be able to produce a digital audio output.

We double-checked the modulation of the transmitter with an oscilloscope. We also double-checked the modulation of the internal reference carrier on the exciter. No overmodulation in the negative direction was observed. Harris had us retune and desensitize the output monitor on the DX-50, and the transmitter then ran fine. I do know that the protection afforded the DX-50 by the output monitor was not compromised, as we took several lightning strikes and did, in fact, have an antenna system problem while this transmitter and exciter combination was on the air, and the transmitter protected itself just as it was supposed to.

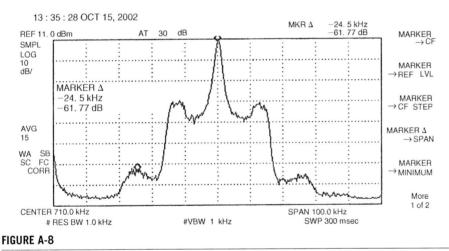

FIGURE A-8

The spectrum of the iBiquity test exciter installation at the old WOR Lyndhurst facility.

At that time, WOR did not have stereo capability in its studios. Therefore, our audio was monaural, feeding both the left and right channels of the exciter with the same material.

The original audio codec was well, it was OK. It wasn't anything to write home about, but it did sound better than standard analog AM radio.

I went to the transmitter site several times in the evenings, after the HD Radio signal was shut off (per FCC regulations at that time), and fed the digital audio processor with stereo music from a CD player, using a test radio from iBiquity to monitor the sample output of the exciter. The audio was well, it was OK. Once again, nothing to write home about, but it was

FIGURE A-9

When WOR put its HD Radio signal on the air with the iBiquity test exciter, the station had old Pacific Recorders and Engineering System 1 consoles – and they were mono. But, the output was clean and provided good test audio.

definitely a different sound than analog AM radio. It was during this experimentation that I discovered a big problem with the first codec.

I like to push systems for all they are worth. So the music I was testing with had great stereo imaging. And, I brought along things like Beatles songs where the vocal is on one channel while the instrumentation is on the other. These songs just didn't sound right on the digital channel.

Suspecting leakage between left and right channels, I put WOR's audio back on the exciter. It sounded fine in digital. Then, I removed one channel of audio, so the exciter was being fed left channel only with nothing on the right channel. Bingo! The left channel sounded OK. The right channel, which should have been dead, had what sounded like splatter from the left channel in it, and this splatter was 26 dB from program level. As long as both channels were being fed the same material, the digital audio sounded fine. As soon as there was a significant difference in what each channel was being fed, the codec was producing artifacts. This was unacceptable.

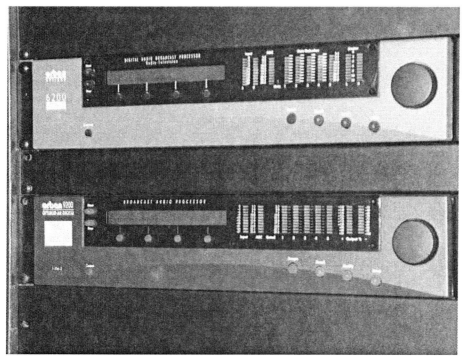

FIGURE A-10

Orban audio processors were used in the original HD Radio installation at WOR. The top unit is an Orban 6200, used to process the digital audio signal. The bottom unit is an Orban 9200, used to process the analog signal.

It should be noted, however, that the analog audio on WOR was unaffected by this.

Several weeks after informing iBiquity of this phenomenon, and demonstrating it for them, they brought out a new load of software for the exciter. This load contained the HDC codec that is presently being used. It was night and day over the original codec, and it eliminated the artifact production with single channel audio.

Over the course of operation of WOR with the iBiquity test exciter, several things were observed which resulted in changes to the system for commercial production. One day, the DX-50 popped off the air, and we could not restart it. We put the auxiliary transmitter on the air and went to the transmitter site.

There, we found the exciter running – fat, dumb, and happy. Or so it appeared. The DX-50, however, was showing that it had lost its RF input. Checking the output of the exciter showed that it was not putting out RF.

In theory, if the exciter failed, the interface box on top of the DX-50 was supposed to switch the transmitter back to analog-only mode. But, as it turned out, the box needed to be told that the exciter was in trouble by the exciter itself. Unfortunately, the exciter didn't know it was in trouble, so the box never received a trouble signal from the exciter and therefore never switched. This resulted in the addition of RF sensing in the exciter monitoring protocol. If the RF output of the exciter quits, regardless of what the exciter actually thinks it is doing at any given time, the transmitter will now revert back to analog-only operation immediately.

I mentioned the iBiquity test radio in a previous paragraph. For the first two years of operation, the only way we could listen to the digital audio on WOR was with an iBiquity test radio. We had one at the transmitter for monitoring, and one at the studio for monitoring. This test radio was also a computer running the Linux operating system. It weighed about 15–20 pounds, and was in a sizeable case. It was not what you would call portable, and required a connection to an AC power outlet to operate.

For the most part, this exciter ran well. It was on the air at WOR from October 11, 2002, until the day we took the Lyndhurst, New Jersey, facility off the air in favor of a new transmitter facility built in Rutherford, New Jersey, on September 8, 2006. This exciter would usually need to be rebooted roughly every six months.

If we did not reboot the exciter roughly every six months, it would slowly start to fail, eventually just locking up, forcing a switch back to analog-only operation. We found we could tell when the exciter was starting its spiral downward by using the graphical user interface, or GUI, to check on any alarms in the system. If the GUI was sluggish, it was time for a reboot. WOR is now using Harris DexStar™ exciters. They tend not to exhibit this problem.

One time we had the exciter start to fail, and it locked up on the analog side. This lock up caused an interesting thing to happen. The analog audio was repeating the 8.4 seconds of audio that aired right before the exciter locked up. Over and over and over. We were able to force the system to analog-only mode with the remote control to restore normal audio to the air. It should be noted that this particular phenomenon happened only once.

A.2 Signal coverage

During the first two years of operation with an HD Radio signal on WOR, we, of course, were curious as to the coverage we were getting with the digital channel. IBiquity, obviously, was interested as well.

FIGURE A-11

WOR's new facility uses Harris 3DX-50 transmitters and Harris DexStar exciters. The exciters are in the rack between the transmitters.

Without a radio, however, it made my attempt at discovering our digital coverage a tad difficult. I did have the iBiquity test radio, but that would have required either a generator or inverter to tote around in the car, and that wouldn't work well.

IBiquity had a van outfitted for monitoring. This van contained an iBiquity test radio that was set up to output data to a mapping computer. The mapping computer kept data on the position of the van through GPS. It also had a data input from a spectrum analyzer, and would log spectrum shots along with information such as data errors, actual digital capture by the radio, and received signal strength. So I had no doubt that the information iBiquity would provide would be fairly accurate.

iBiquity ran test after test, and finally gave me a map showing our digital coverage in several major directions. We had coverage in our secondary lobe to the city line of Philadelphia (and, in fact, we listened to WOR's digital audio at the NAB Radio Show in Philadelphia). We had coverage up

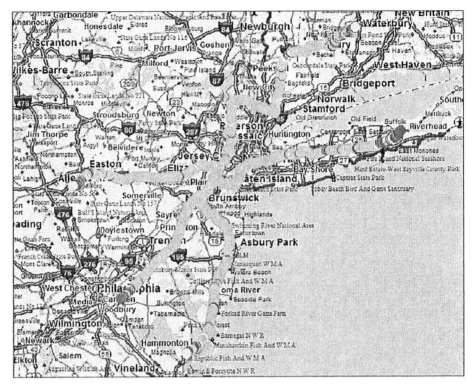

FIGURE A-12

This map of New York and the surrounding area was produced by iBiquity Digital Corporation. It shows the digital coverage of WOR Radio along various routes.

to almost Allentown, Pennsylvania, to the west, which skirts the side of the secondary lobe, but isn't quite in a null. We had coverage to three-fourth the way out on Long Island, which is good, as the ground conductivity over Long Island is awful. The map showed coverage to Waterbury, Connecticut, along I-84 to the north, and also showed coverage just beyond the New York/New Jersey border on route 17. Of course, the naysayers said that the map was fabricated by iBiquity.

When I received my first HD Radio, I took a drive along the same routes iBiquity used to determine the digital coverage of WOR. The radio is a Kenwood and includes the HD Radio module. It was installed in my Ford Explorer and used the stock radio antenna with which the vehicle was equipped.

The map provided by iBiquity turned out to be pretty darn accurate. Where the map said the radio would blend to analog, it did. Where the map said the radio would have digital coverage, it did. Where the map said digital coverage would stop, it did.

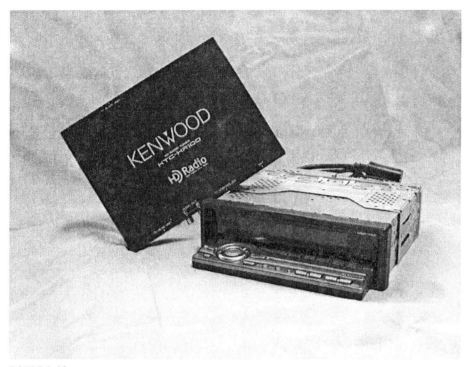

FIGURE A-13

The Kenwood HD Radio car receiver used to check coverage of the WOR signal.

I brought along a Potomac Instruments field intensity meter with me on my drive, and purposely made a signal level measurement when I finally lost digital coverage. Digital coverage was lost between 0.5 and 0.7 mV/m in every direction. At this point, the WOR analog signal was fairly noisy. This, basically, is at a point where I think most listeners would consider the signal too noisy to listen to in analog. I consider the coverage to be good.

In NYC, as you can imagine, there are many areas where an analog AM signal is noisy, at best. There are many places where the WOR signal is barely listenable.

The coverage in the City for the WOR HD Radio signal is rather impressive. I recall the moment when I was taking a reporter for a car magazine around for a driving test of both FM and AM HD Radio signals. We took a

FIGURE A-14

The WOR digital audio dropped out right before this toll booth along the Pennsylvania Turnpike, I-78 in Allentown, Pennsylvania.

path for both signals that took us up the West Side Highway, getting off at the 72nd Street exit and driving through Central Park behind a rock formation, then down 5th Avenue to 34th Street, then heading west to the West Side Highway again. We drove this path four times: once listening to the analog FM signal, once listening to the digital FM signal, once listening to the WOR analog signal, and one last time listening to the WOR digital signal.

While you might not think it, FM signals in NYC tend to suffer from severe multipath distortion. The reason is all the reflections between the buildings. On the West Side Highway, the Empire State Building, home to most of the FM transmitters in NYC, is shielded from view by buildings. You also have reflections off the Hudson River to contend with.

On the analog FM drive, it was obvious up the West Side Highway that the FM signal was annoying to listen to with all the picket-fencing going on. It would clear up slightly until we hit the rock formation in Central Park, when the multipath would start up again, then it would clear up driving down 5th Avenue and on 34th Street.

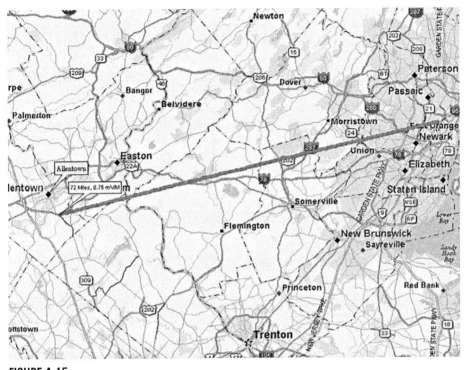

FIGURE A-15

A map showing where the WOR digital signal dropped, just outside of Allentown, PA, 72 miles from the WOR transmitter site.

The digital drive produced a perfect audio signal. No multipath. No noise of any kind.

With the AM signal, the same path would find the analog signal noisy on 34th Street, good on the West Side Highway, sketchy along 72nd Street and through Central Park, and OK along 5th Avenue. The digital drive produced great audio. No dropouts, no noise, and no degradation of any type.

After we finished, the reporter asked me if I would drive him back to his office. We headed east on 40th Street to pick up 2nd Avenue and head north. As we approached Lexington Avenue, I almost panicked. The corner of Lexington and 40th Street has a large building on each corner, which forms a box. I recalled driving with iBiquity and observing on a spectrum analyzer that the entire AM broadcast band would disappear into the noise and, on the night of testing with iBiquity, we would lose the digital signal and end up listening to a noisy analog AM signal.

As we approached Lexington, the light turned red and I was forced to stop in the box formed by the buildings. Interestingly, the radio was still

FIGURE A-16

There are several tunnels connecting Manhattan to the outside world. The Lincoln Tunnel has a "leaky coax" system, which allows motorists to hear AM signals while in the tunnel under the Hudson River. The system does not pass an HD Radio signal, but the change from the coax system to the HD Radio signal when you emerge from the tunnel is dramatic.

producing a digital signal from WOR. The reporter asked me what the analog signal sounded like there, as he noticed we were boxed in. So, I forced the radio to analog mode.

We were greeted with a lot of noise, with barely any audio. Frankly, we could not understand the analog signal. I reset the radio for digital mode and – much to my surprise – the digital signal kicked right in. Needless to say, this was an impressive test for AM HD Radio.

A.3 Nighttime AM HD Radio testing

In December 2002, I participated in nighttime testing of AM IBOC with iBiquity on the signals of WOR, New York, and WLW, Cincinnati.

Both WOR and WLW obtained Special Temporary Authority from the FCC to operate our HD Radio signals at night during this test period. For

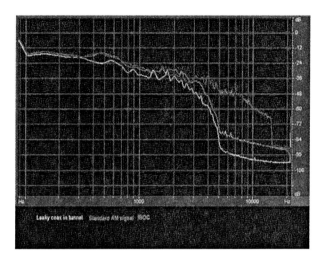

FIGURE A-17

This audio spectral graph was made from a recording I had made of the WOR signal in the Lincoln Tunnel. It shows the frequency response differences in the received audio on the leaky coax system, the off air analog signal, and the off air digital signal.

these tests, iBiquity installed a special load of their software on the exciters at both WOR and WLW. The software was set up to turn the HD Radio subcarriers on for 10 minutes, then turn them off for 10 minutes. The software was synchronized between the stations so that, if the WOR HD Radio signal was on, the WLW signal would be off, and vice versa.

I wrote an article for *Radio Magazine* titled "Three Nights in an iBiquity Van." The unedited version is given in the following paragraphs.

WOR Radio, the 50,000 watt monster in NYC, adopted the iBiquity HD Radio (IBOC) system, and officially became New York's first digital AM radio station at 9 AM, October 11, 2002. WOR was initially chosen as a test station for IBOC, as iBiquity was looking for a blowtorch of a signal near a large city for testing of IBOC coverage and compatibility. Buckley Broadcasting feels that IBOC can only help AM radio, and formally adopted IBOC transmission on WOR the day after it was approved by the FCC.

Thus far, there have been many positives in our transition to IBOC. First and foremost is our daytime digital coverage. WOR has been purposely running our IBOC signal −6 dB from where it should be at the suggestion of iBiquity. The secondary lobe of our directional pattern puts 85,000 watts toward Philadelphia from our transmitter site in Lyndhurst, New Jersey, 95 miles away. Running at −6 dB, our digital coverage, solid, goes as far as the Philadelphia city line, our ½ mV/m boundary. But the $64,000 question is: what would our nighttime IBOC coverage be like, and what would the sideband interference be like?

On the evenings of December 2–5, 2002, I found out while riding around the New York metropolitan area in an iBiquity test van with Russ Mundschenk of iBiquity. There were three nights of testing to perform. The first night was for analog compatibility. The second night was for digital coverage with an IBOC interfering station. The final night was for nighttime digital coverage without an IBOC interferer. The station which would play the role of interferer was WLW, first adjacent station to WOR on 700 kHz, with WOR at 710 kHz.

For compatibility, we drove west out I-78 to a point 51.7 miles from the WOR transmitter site. It was at this point where WLW's skywave, as referenced to WOR's carrier, was −10 dB on an average. This was measured with an HP spectrum analyzer mounted in the iBiquity van, connected to a 31-inch whip antenna on the roof. The location we chose was the parking area of a state highway maintenance area, away from the streetlights. This location proved to be very noise free, and the skywave conditions couldn't be better at 10 PM. The spectrum analyzer, set to show stations from 660 kHz to 770 kHz, showed carriers neatly spaced every 10 kHz. What was really amazing was seeing the skywave phenomenon happen on the spectrum analyzer. You always hear it on a radio while listening to one station, but to actually see only one station that can be affected by atmospherics while the others remain the same is fascinating. The signal from WOR was measured with a Potomac FIM-41, and found to be approximately 0.75 mV/m, roughly WOR's 0.5 mV contour, which was outside the secondary lobe but not yet in the null at 342 degrees. The WOR signal was fairly constant, indicating a ground wave signal. The WLW signal would vary greatly at times, indicating it was sky wave.

The IBOC exciters at WLW and WOR were set so that, for a 10-minute span, WLW's IBOC carriers were on for 1 minute, off for 1 minute, and in this 10-minute time period we monitored WOR. We then changed our monitoring to WLW while WOR's IBOC carriers were toggled on and off in the same sequence. We used six radios to monitor these signals. Five were standard consumer models that you would find at Best Buy, and included a home Technics tuner and a GE SuperRadio III. The sixth was an iBiquity test receiver.

It was my observation that when the WLW carrier was −10 dB as referenced to WOR, and WLW's IBOC carriers were on, there was minor noise under the WOR signal: minor to the effect that the radios needed to be turned up to hear it. If WLW's carrier met or exceeded WOR's carrier level (and WLW exceeded WOR by +10 dB at times), the noise level came up under WOR's signal, but it was far from objectionable. Clearly, the WOR analog signal within our 0.5-mV contour would be useful.

Conversely, when WOR's IBOC carriers were on, and WLW's carrier was −10 dB, the WLW signal was rather noisy. Not to the point of tuning them out, particularly if you were a fan of the basketball team's game being broadcast, but it was annoying nonetheless. If WLW's signal decreased beyond about −15 dB, their signal was pretty much unlistenable. If, however, WLW's signal level were equal to or exceeded WOR's signal level, the noise was only slightly audible and the signal was very useable. It should be noted that when the WLW signal was unlistenable and WOR's IBOC carriers went off, the WLW signal was still unlistenable due to either a station at 700 kHz coming in under them, or sidebands from a station at 690 kHz splashing them. As a generality, I would say that it was not strictly the IBOC carriers that made the signal unlistenable.

After an hour, we packed up and drove to a location about 72 miles from the WOR transmitter, near Bethlehem, Pennsylvania. At this point, the WOR and WLW signals were pretty equal, and judging from the signal variations on the spectrum analyzer, they were both predominantly sky wave. It was found that when both signals were sky wave, the noise level on the desired signal was somewhat annoying when the interfering carrier was −10 dB. The noise level increased if the interferer increased equal to or exceeding the desired carrier, but I considered the signals to be listenable. Annoying, but listenable.

The following night, we took four routes: one took us out I-78, another took us south down the Garden State Parkway, a third took us through Manhattan, through the Queens Midtown Tunnel, and east out the Long Island Expressway, and a fourth took us up WOR's null north on New Jersey Route 17.

The digital signal held out and finally fell apart 50 miles to the west, 52 miles to the south (which was in WOR's minor null), 53 miles to the east on Long Island (which is in the major lobe, but the ground conductivity on Long Island leaves much to be desired), and 20 miles up through our null. It was interesting to note that, driving through our null, the farther we were from the transmitter, the less upper sideband WOR had. Yet the digital signal still decoded, and in general fell apart close to the 0.5-mV/m contour.

In Manhattan, we drove straight down 40th Street. There are several areas on 40th Street before Broadway where the WOR analog signal is fairly noisy. The digital held up. The only place we had an issue was at the corner of 40th Street and Lexington. There are several large buildings here, and it must be a combination of reflections and shielding, but the entire AM band from 660 to 770 kHz as shown on the spectrum analyzer all but disappeared. Of course, no signal, no digital or analog. Coming out from this area, the digital locked right in again.

The Lincoln Tunnel and Queens Midtown Tunnel employ a leaky coax system where the Metropolitan Transportation Authority (MTA) can insert traffic advisories on all NYC AM stations. This system completely stripped off the IBOC sidebands. However, sitting under the roof at the toll plazas at both tunnels, the digital kept cranking.

The last night, testing was done with only WOR's IBOC on. Coverage was substantially the same as with WLW as an IBOC interferer, leading one to believe that this interference does not affect an IBOC signal.

Quite frankly, listening to the digital on the road was quite amazing. Joey Reynolds had a guest singing live Christmas Carols with an acoustic guitar, and it almost sounded like the guy were in the van with us, it was that good. It was also amazing, realizing this was an AM station, and it wasn't fuzzing up under bridges and overpasses.

My opinion is that, if the IBOC carriers were backed down from -3 to $-6\,$dB at night, the digital coverage would be less, but there would be less impact on analog signals. Certainly, digital coverage is adequate at night on the WOR signal.

Another thought is this. If you put up a Class-B FM station, you expect to lose signal once you reach about 50 miles out, depending on terrain. No one bats an eye. Maybe we should start considering AM in this same vein. The audio quality of the digital signal, in my opinion, far surpasses the analog quality. Is IBOC the savior AM radio has been in search of? I don't know. But I do know that, personally, I would rather have the digital audio to listen to rather than the bandwidth-restricted scratchy analog. But that's not up to me to decide. And that's why WOR is testing, and proud to be HD.

A.4 Nighttime hybrid AM HD Radio operation

On September 14, 2007, it became legal to operate the HD Radio signal at night on AM radio stations in the United States. WOR turned its HD Radio signal on at 12:01 AM on the morning of September 14, the time it became legal to do so.

The decision to allow nighttime AM HD Radio operation by the FCC was a bold move – and fit in with the wording of their Report and Order on the creation of IBOC rules. The reason it was a bold move was that, while many studies of nighttime AM HD Radio operation have been done (the WOR/WLW tests being just one of them), exactly what would happen when many AM HD Radio signals were lit up at night was somewhat of an unknown.

The hybrid AM HD Radio signal is designed to provide digital coverage out to a station's 0.5-mV/m contour daytime – and at night if conditions allow. It is designed so that, with the station spacing and regulations in the United States, it should not infringe upon the 2-mV/m nighttime interference-free contour of a neighboring adjacent station. There are, of course, some exceptions to this, but they are relatively few.

And herein lies the controversy with nighttime AM HD Radio operation. Many people mistakenly think that an AM radio station's coverage is wherever you can hear it. That is wrong. The FCC rules define the coverage contours of AM radio stations. They also define contours where you can expect to receive and not receive interference to your signal. And it is important to note that these contours are based on carrier frequency – not on modulation. And on the basis of this information, it becomes clear that these coverage contours are used to determine spacing between stations.

Section 73.44 of the FCC rules defines your occupied spectrum – in other words, how much space your modulated signal can take up. Under Section 73.44, the hybrid AM HD Radio signal is perfectly legal. In actuality, you could modulate the AM transmitter with broadband noise, tailored by an equalizer to fit under the mask defined in Section 73.44 – and your station would be legal. Adjacent stations may not be happy with you, but you would be legal under the FCC regulations. Contours and occupied bandwidth are two things that some persons simply do not understand.

That being said, on the morning when nighttime HD Radio operation was legal, many of us were greeted by complaint e-mails. These e-mails were generated by frustrated DXers who, they claim, could no longer listen to certain stations because of an adjacent HD Radio station.

I received one from a guy in Maryland, and was actually going to take this guy seriously until I hit the anti-IBOC rhetoric in his note. He claimed that the WOR signal was wiping out reception of both WLW and WGN at his home.

I called a friend in Maryland who happened to live two towns over from where this guy stated he lived. My friend had been up at 1 AM – and purposely listened to 700 kHz, 710 kHz, and 720 kHz. He said he heard no problems and had no trouble at all listening to WLW or WGN at his home. I would tend to believe my friend.

I live near Newburgh, New York, about 50 miles due north of NYC. I have listened on my car radio, on a C. Crane CCRadio Plus using its internal antenna, and on my Yaesu FT-857D Ham rig using a 110-foot dipole antenna. I am specifically interested in how the analog signals of adjacent stations are affected by IBOC operation. In the following paragraphs, my observations of nighttime HD Radio operation are given, with the HD Radio stations in italic type.

700 WLW, 710 WOR, 720 WGN – I live in WOR's null, and WOR's signal is normally very noisy at my home. It did not get noisier. The signal still sounds the same, with the exception of about an hour before sunrise when the signal does get noisier. It should be noted that WOR's signal level in my driveway is 0.3 mV/m. I have no trouble listening to WLW or WGN, and have listened to them closer in to WOR's transmitter. When the WOR signal is over 2 mV/m, WLW and WGN do get noisy. But, this is outside their 2-mV/m contours.

800 CKLW, *810 WGY*, 820 Station not identified – I live about 100 miles south of WGY's Schenectady, New York, transmitter site. CKLW comes screaming in here like a local at night and is perfectly listenable. WGY sounds fine. I can hear a station on 820, noisy but not IBOC noise, but it is there.

1530 WCKY, *1540 WDCD*, 1550 Station not identified – I live about 100 miles south of WDCD's Albany, New York, transmitter site, and I am in somewhat of a null of their signal. I have no problems hearing WCKY, and no problems hearing one of the several stations on 1550.

1070 CBA, *1080 WTIC*, 1090 WBAL – I live about 100 miles from WTIC's transmitter. WTIC is allowed to remain 50,000 Watts, nondirectional until two hours past sunset, so after sunset, WTIC is still pumping a full 50 kW in my direction. On their night pattern, I would receive considerably less signal. WTIC comes in like a local. CBA, while weak, is there and perfectly listenable. WBAL just screams up into this area, and actually shows more signal on my Ham rig than WTIC does, and is perfectly listenable.

1100 WTAM, *1110 WBT*, 1120 KMOX – I can hear all three stations with no problems.

760 WJR, 770 WABC, 780 WBBM – I am about 46 miles due north of the WABC transmitter in Lodi, New Jersy. WABC puts greater than 2 mV/m at my home. The WABC signal was clear. WJR was difficult to listen to, as it was very noisy, but it could be heard. The same case is with WBBM.

It should be noted that, to my knowledge, none of these stations is experiencing a problem with their signal inside their 2-mV/m contours.

While some distant listeners are experiencing problems with their hobby, I do not believe that most listeners have noticed any difference in the signals of their favorite stations since the inception of nighttime AM HD Radio operation. There are, of course, exceptions. But overall, I do not think there is a major problem. The nighttime AM radio landscape has begun to change.

A.5 Practical considerations for the implementation of AM IBOC

The text in the next paragraph in this section is a paper I prepared and delivered for the NAB show in 2003. It is basically the opening story of this chapter as it was presented to National Association of Broadcasters (NAB).

INTRODUCTION: After many years of development, the time to begin implementation of IBOC digital transmission on the AM band has arrived. For some, it will be an expensive proposition.

WOR-AM in NYC was approached by iBiquity Digital Corporation in regards to becoming a test station for IBOC-AM. We agreed and, while the final software load for the exciter was not yet ready, WOR turned IBOC on and committed to it on a permanent basis on October 11, 2002, the day after the FCC approved the use of IBOC. On this day, WOR became New York's first digital AM radio station.

This paper serves to inform you of some of the practical considerations for implementing AM IBOC at your facility. We will discuss what WOR did and did not do to implement IBOC, and we will discuss some of our findings that you might not have thought of.

WHAT YOUR STATION NEEDS TO IMPLEMENT IBOC: Unfortunately, there has not been a plethora of information available on the implementation of IBOC. If you go by the information in ads in the trade publications, it appears that you need to have a digital studio sources feeding a digital console, which feeds a digital STL, a digital processor, and an IBOC exciter and your transmitter. About the only thing I haven't seen in the ads is that you should also have a digital announcer.

When WOR implemented IBOC, we were using original, 1978 vintage Pacific Recorders and Engineering System One consoles. They were mono and they still sounded pretty good. While 2003 was going to herald a reconfiguration of the WOR facility, WOR was still using the System One consoles in October 2002. And if you look around the typical WOR control room, you find a rather eclectic mix of older technology and new technology. Everything from turntables, which are used during the Joe Franklin program on Saturday night (and Joe still brings 78-RPM records in to play), to an ENCO system. I would think that the WOR studio situation is fairly typical of most stations in the United States.

To sum up our studio situation with the implementation of IBOC, WOR feeds analog audio into an older analog console. The consoles were in reasonable shape and had reasonable specifications that were still being met. There was no immediate need to go out and immediately purchase five brand new completely digital consoles. If your consoles are still in reasonable shape and sound good, there should be no need to replace your consoles to implement IBOC. The reason WOR is reconfiguring our studios, which will include new consoles, is that most of the semiconductors and switches used in these consoles are no longer available. If they were not next to impossible to repair, we would most likely be keeping the PR&E consoles for another few years.

Our Master Control room contains passive relay studio switchers, which are stereo. Presently, the right channel is used to switch paths for the cue tones used for the WOR Radio Networks. As part of taking WOR stereo over the next few months, these switchers will be added onto so that we have a different path that will follow the main switchers for the cue tones. At the present time, there is no need to change a set of studio switchers that still work fine and we can still obtain parts for.

One reason that the reconfiguration of the WOR facility will maintain analog audio is our top-hour time tone. I have yet to find anyone who makes a small, rack-mountable, two-channel stereo mixer so that we can maintain the automatic insertion of our time tone. Deleting the time tone is not an option, as it has been on WOR for decades, and is actually constructed using a middle-C oscillator module from a Hammond organ. Many times during the day WOR is automated, sometimes we are live, and automatic insertion of the time tone is a must. So for this aspect, WOR must maintain analog audio through the studio switchers.

Once the audio passes through an Orban 8200ST processor, it is fed through a distribution amplifier to feed our STL paths. WOR maintains five STL paths to our transmitter in New Jersey. The first is an Intraplex STL/TSL unit that transmits bidirectionally on a Harris Aurora 5.8-GHz spread spectrum radio. This allows us to bring back our satellite channels from Jersey to Manhattan, gives us a 15-kHz nondata reduced path to the transmitter in stereo, plus allows for five data channels and two telco paths between the transmitter and studio. Because the Intraplex rack is utilizing all the time slots on the T1 created with the Aurora, we could not put Intraplex's "IBOC" card into the unit and maintain our data and telco channels. This means that the WOR audio goes into and comes out of the Intraplex analog, and is 15-kHz bandwidth. We did not see a reason to increase the bandwidth to 20 kHz, as the IBOC will pass up to 15 kHz.

Our second STL is a 950-band Moseley DSP-6000, which is stereo. While this uses data reduction, it is perfectly adequate as a second stereo backup for WOR.

Our third STL is a 950-band mono Moseley PCL-6010 transmitter and 6020 receiver. Once again, as a third backup, this STL is perfectly adequate and did not need to be replaced.

Our fourth path is an 8-kHz equalized phone line which, at times, has been known to hum or whistle quietly. Once again, if we need to resort to the phone line, it is better than the alternatives (i.e., the sounds of silence), and this STL path will be adequate even with IBOC.

Our final STL path is a G.722 ISDN codec, which is intended for extreme emergency use, such as if we needed to abandon the Manhattan studios and broadcast from elsewhere. Under these circumstances, this path would be more than adequate even with IBOC.

Bottom line, I saw no good reason to replace our studio switchers or STLs with a completely digital path. What we are using sounds good, is reliable, and is perfectly adequate with our IBOC installation. If your analog audio path to the transmitter sounds good and is reliable, there should be no immediate need to go through the expense of replacing your STLs. And while stereo would be nice, if they're mono, so what? Your present signal is mono. Aim for stereo STLs sometime down the road.

At the transmitter, by necessity due to our need to feed analog audio to our auxiliary transmitter chain, the audio that comes out of our various STL paths is analog, and goes through a passive Broadcast Tools switcher. The WOR transmitter site was rewired in 1997, and I wired it with stereo in mind. The output of the switcher feeds a distribution amplifier, which feeds the auxiliary transmitter chain, still feeds the main chain with an analog signal, and now also feeds an analog-to-digital (A/D) converter. The IBOC equipment requires an AES digital signal. The A/D converter takes the analog audio from the STL switcher and converts it to an AES signal before the ESU unit of the IBOC exciter. If you intend to keep your STL path analog, you will need to purchase an A/D converter. Ours is from Radio Systems.

In addition to certain control aspects it has over the IBOC exciter, the ESU also acts as an AES distribution amplifier. It feeds our Optimod 9200 an AES signal for the analog processing of our signal, and feeds our Optimod 6200 an AES signal for the IBOC portion of our signal. The processor for your analog signal should have AES in and out, as the IBOC exciter accepts AES in only for either the analog or digital signals. And you will need to purchase a separate processor for the IBOC audio. The processor you choose should have digital broadcasting in mind, though an FM processor with the pre-emphasis defeated should work fine. This processor also needs to be AES in and out.

There are a few paths to take when connecting the IBOC exciter to your transmitter. One is to simply connect the exciter and turn it on. The one chosen by WOR was to connect a relay to the IBOC transmitter to exciter interface unit, in addition to our analog output of the Optimod 9200. If the IBOC exciter were to fail, the relay drops out and switches the RF input to our DX-50 transmitter back to the internal oscillator. Having our analog Optimod output available through the interface box (which contains an audio relay) would cause the transmitter's audio input to change from the IBOC exciter's output to the standard output from the Optimod. This would keep WOR on the air in the event of an exciter failure, and it proved to be the correct decision one morning when, after running a special program on the exciter to switch the IBOC carriers on and off for testing, the exciter spontaneously rebooted when I attempted to kill the toggling program. The DX-50 simply dumped when the RF input switched, and came right back up after about one second. No issues, no lost time.

Now that you know that the exciter is a computer, running the IBOC program under Linux, how is the power at your site? You should put the exciter, the D/A converter, and the processors, as a minimum, on a good uninterruptable power supply that is the type which is always on line and has surge protection. This will help prevent the Linux computer from locking up with power hits.

Another consideration with the exciter is the interconnection to the transmitter. The RF and audio or, as they are known in IBOC lingo, the phase and magnitude signals exit the exciter on RJ-45 connectors. The connection between the exciter and the interface box in your transmitter should be shielded Cat-5 cable. The connection between the interface box and the transmitter should be an RG-58 cable terminated in BNC connectors for the RF, and regular single-pair shielded audio cable for the magnitude connection, and terminated in spade lugs for the transmitter, and bare wires for the Phoenix-type connectors on the interface box. You will need to determine how your transmitter will accept the external RF input and plan a relay accordingly if you intend to add the fail-safe switching described earlier. In the WOR installation, we discovered during installation that our supplier shipped nonshielded RJ-45 connectors in a package marked that they were shielded. We simply took the shield wires on the Cat-5, crimped spade lugs on the ends, and attached them to the nearest screw with a ground connection. Whatever works.

Your transmitter is going to be a big consideration. IBOC will not work with a plate-modulated transmitter. It is questionable if it will work with a tube pulse duration modulation (PDM) transmitter, and will not work with a Doherty modulated transmitter. The Harris DX series of transmitter, of which WOR has a DX-50, is pretty much plug and play for IBOC. Broadcast Electronics and Nautel transmitters are likewise.

If you have a PDM transmitter that is solid state, you will need to check with the manufacturer to see if the transmitter will pass IBOC. Most transmitters have a modification kit available, as the audio passband must be 50 kHz through the PDM modulator. Most likely the PDM frequency and the PDM filtering sections will need to be changed out. Your transmitter needs to have a pretty flat audio response that is 50-kHz wide, and the RF section needs to have a fairly low amount of phase noise, or, as we know it from AM stereo days, Incidental Quadrature Modulation (IQM) or incidental phase modulation (IPM). You should check with the manufacturer and make a decision as to whether you should purchase a new transmitter.

Your antenna is the other big consideration. WOR employs a three-tower dogleg directional array. There are detuning skirts, two on each tower, for 1010 (WINS) and 1190 (WLIB) to electrically shorten the WOR towers at these frequencies. The tuning houses have detuning networks for 1010, 1190, and 620 (WJWR), in addition to traps for 1010, 1190, and 620. To say that our array is "challenging" for a fairly flat path at and about 710 kHz is an understatement.

We had Tom Jones from the firm Carl T. Jones Corporation redesign our coupling networks and phasor in 1997. By putting line stretchers in each tuning house, making all the tuning networks phase lead (there had been one phase lag previously), and changing a few components in the phasor, as well as changing the common point from 75 ohms to 50 ohms, the WOR common point is now fairly flat, both resistance and reactance, from 690 to 730, ideal for IBOC. The lower sideband is favored slightly, and this can be seen in the lower IBOC sideband being about 1.5 dB higher than the upper IBOC sideband.

The load presented to your transmitter needs to be fairly flat ±15 kHz from carrier in both resistance and reactance. At the very least, if asymmetry is present, the impedance needs to be asymmetric equally and opposite on both sides of carrier. You should sweep your system to see what the transmitter is actually looking into. You may need to hire a consultant to flatten things out. If WOR's system could be flattened, there is indeed hope for your system.

OTHER CONSIDERATIONS: In addition to the technical considerations mentioned previously, there are a few other considerations that we learned with our foray into IBOC. The first revolves around the inherent approximate 8.5-second delay introduced into the analog audio once you have converted to IBOC. The reason for this delay is that the radios are designed to blend back to analog should the digital signal encounter a problem. This prevents the audio from going away rather abruptly. Obviously, if you do not delay the analog 8.5 seconds, this blend will be choppy at best.

WOR is a talk station and, consequently, operates with a profanity delay most of the time. The exceptions are the top-of-the-hour newscasts and portions of The WOR Morning Show. Obviously, the talent cannot monitor air when air is delayed by 8.5 seconds. To counter this, we changed the air-monitoring position in all studios to feed off the directional antenna (DA) that feeds the STLs. This gave the talent a real time audio feed of the audio before it left for Jersey.

The problem with this is that the air talent were used to hearing the signal all "pumped up" and heavily processed. Some had trouble adjusting to the cleaner, flatter signal. To correct this, we took an old CRL AM system that had occupied rack space at the transmitter and inserted it into the feed the studios were getting. This gave the talent their pumped up audio and made them happy.

The next problem to resolve was: if you can't listen to air (even in the Master Control room), how do you know if you're on the air? Oh, you'll know if the transmitter is on the air. WOR has computer monitors in each control room that displays the transmitter status at a glance. But what about an audio failure?

We installed two silence sensors. One on the feed into the studio to transmitter link (STL) transmitters, the other on the analog modulation monitor. They are set for 10 seconds. If either the feed to the STL quits (i.e., somebody switches to a dead studio) or the transmitter audio quits (i.e., STL failure or processor failure), the thing screams. We should bless Radio Shack for having loud, obnoxious piezo beepers available. There are also silence sensors at the transmitter site feeding status lights on the remote control. If the silence sensor goes off, a simple glance at the transmitter screen will show if it's at the transmitter site or studio. If the problem is at the transmitter site, the screen will show if it is the active STL receiver or the transmitter where the audio has quit.

Another issue: program on hold on the office phone system. It had been fed off the same DA that feeds the studio monitors. Rick Buckley, our President, observed that the hold audio was 8.5 seconds ahead of what he was hearing on his office radio in Greenwich, Connecticut, and thought it was rather confusing. The program on hold feed now comes from the modulation monitor directly.

What about the time tone? We have people who literally set their watch by the WOR time tone. The switchboard floods with complaints if we patch the time tone out briefly for maintenance. I could just imagine what would happen if it were 8.5 seconds off. Can you say complaints to the FCC for giving erroneous time information? WOR utilizes a programmable timer made by ESE to fire off various things, like the backup feed mini disk machines for The WOR Radio Networks. We programmed a position on this timer to fire the time tone at 59:51.5, so it hits air at exactly straight up on the hour. We have had no complaints.

Live sports? This is an issue that is being worked on by iBiquity. Your station can ramp in and out of the 8.5-second delay but, as mentioned previously, this may cause blend problems between analog and digital signals on radios. iBiquity has told us they are working on setting a bit in the data stream to inform listeners that the analog feed is real time for a live sporting event, and the listener can choose to listen to the digital or analog feed. This will allow persons listening in the stands or watching the game on TV and listening to WOR to hear the game in real time.

One thing that no one considered at WOR was the effect the 8.5-second delay would have on our top hour newscasts. We are formatted to hit the ID/news sounder on top of the hour. At the time IBOC was implemented, the ID cut was 24 seconds long. We normally have a 10 second "brought to you by" announcement at the top of the cast, meaning that we didn't get to the actual lead story until 34 seconds past the hour. Add the 8.5-second delay to the mix, and we now did not get into the lead story until almost 43 seconds past the hour. While WOR is not a news station, this problem came to light on one particularly busy news day, when every station in NYC had already hit the lead story, gone to the outside reporter, and was into the second story before our announcer was even out of the sponsor announcement.

Our solution was to shorten the ID to under 15 seconds, and advance the clocks in the studio complex so that everything would happen 8.5 seconds early. If we were 8.5 seconds early, it would hit air on time. But there were two problems. First, the digital clocks were locked to our GPS receiver and that couldn't be changed. Our ENCO system was also locked to the GPS receiver, meaning that all automation-timed events would need to be reprogrammed. Finally, what would we do about The WOR Radio Networks? They need to feed on a real-time basis. If we advanced the clocks, and an operator made a mistake, we would go up at 06:32 rather than 06:40, or come out at 58:42 rather than 58:50, fouling up hundreds of stations around the country.

The solution came in a product manufactured by Symetrix under the AirTools name. The AirTools digital delay units delay audio, TC-89 time code, and contact closures! By setting an 8.5-second delay on the AirTools unit, the TC-89 time code would advance by a corresponding 8.5 seconds. This would make the digital clocks and the ENCO system correspond to the 8.5 second advance of the analog clocks. This meant that, in real time, the network would start at 06:32, but hit the satellite channel at 06:40 as it should. The only time WOR hits an outside source is with Mutual News from 9PM through 4AM. Only a handful of automation commands would need to be changed. None of the automated records for the network would need to be changed. And WOR would now be on time.

HARRASSMENT: One of the things that no one considered was the reaction of a certain small segment of the community. These people are DXers. Some belong to an AM Stereo club.

My Chief Engineer, Kerry Richards, and myself were verbally attacked on a personal level on at least two very public message boards. We have been harassed via e-mail and on the telephone. I have had people trying to get me to "admit" that I am operating WOR illegally. I am not. WOR's operation is perfectly legal under the FCC regulations. I have been threatened with "I'm going to write a complaint to the FCC regarding your illegal operation." My response has been, "Go right ahead. WOR is operating legally and the FCC is welcome to inspect us at any time. And I would suggest that you should have your facts and documented proof of our illegal operation. The FCC won't follow up unless you have credible evidence."

We have had to have the phone number changed at the transmitter site. If we turned the IBOC on after sunset, even after midnight, the phone had rung and we had met with a stream of obscenities and hung up on. The caller ID was blocked and I had no idea how someone got a nonlisted non-published phone number. It's nice to know that some people have nothing better to do than call radio station transmitter sites … at all hours of the day and night … and harass the engineers.

I have been accused of splattering the AM band from 540 kHz to 1030 kHz. I have had people who tell me that I must protect skywave signals coming into the New York metropolitan area at night: incidentally, there is nothing in the FCC regulations requiring me to do so once outside protected contours.

I haven't been physically threatened at this point, nor has anyone attempted to gain access to the WOR facility. If that day comes, the person or persons involved will find out what happens to them, as the WOR transmitter site plays a big part in New Jersey's Homeland Security disaster plans. The feds will most likely not take too kindly to the WOR facility or engineers being physically threatened.

In short, your station should brace not only for the positive aspects of what IBOC will bring you, but also for the negativity. It's amazing how such a small group can have such big mouths. Your promotion department, if you have one, should have a way to handle these situations. Bottom line, in my opinion, is that IBOC helps AM, and that is why you are considering installing IBOC on your AM facility.

CONCLUSION: These are the things that we at WOR needed to take under consideration in our facility when we committed to IBOC. While these items are by no means a complete list, it should help you to see items that will need consideration before you take your AM station IBOC. Each station and set of circumstances is different, and only you can decide what is the best way to handle the issues that may crop up with IBOC implementation.

With well-thought-out implementation, and the ability to react to issues as they pop up, your transition to IBOC will be smooth and fairly uneventful.

A.6 Real-world AM IBOC coverage using a consumer IBOC radio

The next article below was written in 2004 for presentation at the NAB show, and describes my testing with the Kenwood HD Radio.

INTRODUCTION: WOR-AM radio in NYC became an IBOC test station for iBiquity Digital Corporation in October 2002. WOR-HD, as we call our IBOC operation, also became New York's first digital AM radio station.

Until December of 2003, the only listening that could be done to WOR's IBOC signal was on test radios provided by iBiquity, one at the transmitter facility in Lyndhurst, New Jersey, the other in the Master Control Room of WOR on the 23rd floor of 1440 Broadway in NYC. Taking either of these radios for a test drive was out of the question, as they both required AC power, contained hard disk drives, and would also require an analog-to-digital converter along with outboard amplifier and speakers.

The WOR digital coverage was determined by iBiquity using its test vans. We needed to take its word as to what was our digital coverage, as we had no way to measure it.

AND THEN ALONG COMES A PRODUCTION MODEL RADIO: In December 2003, WOR received an actual production model IBOC-capable radio from Kenwood. The radio consisted of the Kenwood KDC-722 head unit, with the Kenwood KTC-HR100 HD Radio module.

This Kenwood radio was installed into an average 2003 model year Ford Explorer, utilizing an installation kit from Crutchfield Electronics.

The HD Radio module was installed in the glove box of the Explorer utilizing hook and loop fasteners. While there was plenty of room behind the glove box inside the dash board to install this module, it was placed in the glove box to offer ease of access to the RCA output jacks located on this unit for audio recording purposes.

Care was taken to make sure the unit was properly grounded to the frame of the vehicle to minimize any ignition or electrical noise entering the radio and HD module.

While the factory antenna cable was capable of reaching the HD module without a problem, it was decided to install the HD module using the included antenna extension cable. This cable was approximately 12–15 feet in length, and would most likely be used in any consumer installation. We wanted this installation to be most like one the average consumer would undergo at his local auto stereo shop.

LET THE TESTING BEGIN: Testing was to be done along a radial used by iBiquity during their coverage tests. The route chosen was directly out I-78 from Newark, New Jersey. This Interstate runs in almost a straight line at a bearing of 258 degrees true from the WOR transmitter facility in Lyndhurst, New Jersey.

Before beginning the test drive, it was decided to place a magnetic mount whip antenna on top of the vehicle connected to the external antenna input of a Potomac FIM-41 Field Intensity Meter. The WOR monitor points were used to calibrate the antenna with a second FIM-41. Once the FIM connected to the magnetic mount was grounded to the vehicle chassis to provide a ground point, the signal proved stable and remained calibrated for the purposes of this testing at each of the four WOR monitoring point locations.

Leaving the WOR transmitter site showed that the radio's stereo light was on, meaning that the radio was locked on the enhanced IBOC carrier. The route to I-78 went East on Route 3, South on I-95, then heading West on I-78.

The majority of the ride out I-78 found the Kenwood radio locked onto the enhanced mode. There was no blending to analog mode under bridges, though there was a quick blend to analog at one point where I-78 passes through a "concrete canyon," two high concrete walls located on each side of the Interstate. The analog signal at this point was noisy, so it made sense that the radio would blend to analog. The ride was uneventful up to the Pennsylvania border.

Coming up to the toll plaza, the signal would occasionally blend to analog. Pulling over to the side of the road immediately after the toll plaza showed a signal level of 1.4 mV/m at 40 degrees, 35 minutes, 46.6 seconds North latitude and 75 degrees, 20 minutes, 5 seconds West longitude as measured on a GPS, a distance of 66.4 miles from the center of the WOR antenna system at an angle of 258.7 degrees true. This location is just outside Bethlehem, Pennsylvania.

Driving further West showed that, after the toll plaza, the radio had dropped out of enhanced mode, but stayed locked on the digital carrier in core mode. This meant the stereo light was off, but the radio was still receiving a mono digital signal.

At the point where the stereo light no longer flickered on and the radio made its first blend to analog, the vehicle was pulled over and the signal level measured. The signal level was 0.96 mV/m at 40 degrees, 34 minutes, 3.5 seconds North latitude and 75 degrees, 24 minutes, 35 seconds West longitude, a distance of 70.7 miles at a bearing of 257.8 degrees true from the WOR transmitter facility. This location was right outside Allentown, Pennsylvania.

Continuing further West showed that the radio blended to analog permanently at a signal level of 0.75 mV/m at 40 degrees, 33 minutes, 59.9 seconds North latitude and 75 degrees, 29 minutes, 13.7 seconds West longitude, a distance of 74.6 miles at a bearing of 258.4 degrees true from the WOR transmitter.

It appears that, along this radial, WOR's digital coverage takes us to Allentown, Pennsylvania. This is far outside the New York metropolitan area and is perfectly adequate for WOR's needs.

It should be noted that WOR's directional antenna forms a lobe aimed directly toward Philadelphia from Lyndhurst. The radial out to Allentown skirts this lobe to the north, and lies between the center of the lobe and WOR's deepest null.

Comparing this coverage to a map provided by iBiquity, which unfortunately will not reproduce properly for this paper, shows that iBiquity's tests list digital coverage along this radial out to Allentown. It appears that the Kenwood radio works to the iBiquity system design and is providing digital coverage to areas where iBiquity says their system should provide the coverage.

Why does the radio blend to analog at 0.75 mV/m rather than 0.5 mV/m? There could be numerous reasons. Among them: it could be the fact that the Explorer's antenna is 32 inches long instead of a meter in length, it could be the excess antenna cable connected to the HD module, and it could be component tolerances in the front end of the HD module. It could be electrical noise generated by the Explorer. The bottom line, though, is that the coverage experienced with the Kenwood radio is exactly what iBiquity found with their test vans.

FURTHER OBSERVATIONS: The route the author drives into the City each day runs directly near the center of WOR's null. iBiquity predicted that digital coverage would end at the New York/New Jersey border at the intersection of Route 17, I-287, and I-87. This is where our digital coverage ends with the Kenwood radio.

After this location driving South, there are a couple of quick blends to analog, as the WOR signal is shaky in this area. Once through Mahwah, New Jersey, however, the digital coverage is solid down Route 17, over to Route 3, and to the Lincoln Tunnel. It should also be noted that the pattern bandwidth of the WOR signal in the null is not very good. North of Paramus, New Jersey, the WOR upper sideband is greatly diminished. Yet WOR has digital coverage to the predicted location.

Further observations show that, driving cross-town from the outlet of the Lincoln Tunnel down 40th Street to Broadway, the digital coverage in the City is excellent. There are places along this route where the analog signal is very noisy. If a taxi pulls up along side the vehicle, the Radio Frequency Interference (RFI) generated by its taximeter generates a whine in the analog signal.

The Kenwood radio, however, stays locked on the digital carrier. In trouble spots for the analog signal, the digital signal goes to mono core, but it stays digital.

FM OBSERVATIONS: WNEW-FM is transmitting an IBOC carrier from the top of the Empire State Building. While Empire State Building may be the tallest location in the city of New York, reflections caused by the buildings blocking the signal along the West Side cause WNEW-FM's signal to picket-fence with multipath distortion all the way up the West Side Highway from 42nd Street to the George Washington Bridge.

WNEW-FM's IBOC signal is free of this multipath distortion. One can drive up the West Side Highway, hit the button on the radio for WNEW-FM, and hear the analog signal spitting. The radio then blends to digital, and the multipath magically disappears.

While I have not measured signal levels on WNEW-FM, the Kenwood radio appears to hold the digital signal almost to the point where the WNEW-FM analog signal starts having problems.

Overall, from AM measurements to simple FM listening, I would say that this first commercial IBOC radio on the market performs as intended. I don't think the public will be disappointed with the performance of this radio. Kenwood says that they have learned a great deal about the IBOC signal while designing this radio. The second generation of IBOC radios can only be better.

A.7 Installation of IBOC on AM

The following article was written for *Radio World Magazine* in late 2002.

While we've all heard and seen things regarding IBOC digital transmission for AM and FM stations, there hasn't been much written in regards to what it will take to install IBOC on an existing installation. WOR, a 50-kW flame thrower in NYC, and one of America's pioneer broadcasters, became New York's first digital AM radio station at 9 AM, October 11, 2002.

First and foremost, before you delve into the world of IBOC, you must first evaluate your transmitter facility. You may have been seeing articles regarding what you need to do in order to make your facility IBOC ready. Would it be nice to have all-digital studios and a completely digital STL to make this happen? Sure. Is this practical for most stations? No. Most of us need to live within a budget, and replacing the entire plant, microphone to antenna, makes no sense initially. Since this article focuses on the transmitter plant, I'll briefly say that WOR has older studio equipment: our consoles are literally serial numbers 1–5 of PR&E's System 1 console, the predecessor to the BMX, and are mono. We will be concentrating on our studios within the next two to three years, and made no changes at the studio with the exception of our monitoring situation, as IBOC introduced an 8.5-second delay into our analog audio.

IS YOUR TRANSMITTER PLANT READY?: WOR's transmitter facility has seen much work over the past five years. It started with a complete rebuild of the phasor and coupling circuits for our three-tower dogleg array. But this is not just any three tower dogleg.

WOR's transmitter plant is located in Lyndhurst, New Jersey. It is an RF oasis. On our street, all within 1½ miles of each other are: WOR, WLIB, WJWR, and WINS. Counting WOR, there is approximately 300 kW of RF over our site. You shut WOR's transmitter off, ground a tower, and draw a considerable arc. We have almost 3V/m at 1010 (WINS) alone. Needless to say, our antenna system consists of detuning skirts on the towers to electrically shorten them at 1010 and 1190; detuning networks at the bases of the towers for 620, 1010, and 1190; traps for 620, 1010, and 1190; and then we actually get to the components that WOR can use.

The redesign, performed by Cart T. Jones Corporation, took WOR's common point which looked like a roller coaster on either side of 710, and made it fairly flat ±15 kHz from carrier. After that, it goes to hell in a hurry, but for IBOC operation, your antenna and/or common point should look fairly flat and the reactance flat or at least symmetrical over the passband of ±15 kHz from carrier. WOR passed the first major test.

You next need to look at your transmitter. According to information I received from Harris at their IBOC road show, a tube-type AM transmitter pretty much will not have the stability required for the phase modulation components of the IBOC signal. The RF chain needs to be fairly linear, and, in the case of a PDM transmitter, the sampling frequency needs to be high enough and the filtering broad enough to allow the IBOC components to properly pass through to the final.

WOR utilizes a Harris DX-50 transmitter for a main. It is basically plug and play for IBOC. Our older auxiliary transmitter, a Continental 317C-1, pretty much doesn't have a prayer of passing IBOC, though both Chief Engineer Kerry Richards and myself think it might be interesting to try IBOC on the beast to see what would happen. Since WOR had a main transmitter which is more than capable of passing the IBOC signal, and the antenna system looked good, it was time to play.

INSTALLATION: Kerry and I did some preparation at the site before Pat Malley, a field engineer for iBiquity, arrived one fine Sunday afternoon for installation. To get the IBOC signal into the transmitter, there is an interface box that needs to be installed between the exciter and transmitter. The connections between the interface and the transmitter are a BNC for a coax connection to the external RF input and a Phoenix-type connector for the audio connection. As an option, there is a control voltage input that can be paralleled to a relay in the transmitter to change between internal and external excitation.

Connection between the exciter and interface is done with Cat-5. I can now say that I have pretty much seen it all since I have connected my first 50-kW AM rig using shielded Cat-5 cable. Before Pat arrived, Kerry and I had run the Cat-5 from the racks to the transmitter, and made sure we had jacks available on the patch bay for input to the A/D converter. Time to do this was about one hour.

Pat arrived bearing gifts, and we put the auxiliary on the air. We proceeded to connect the Cat-5. Kerry worked on getting the connections between the patchbay, A/D converter, exciter, and processing correct. I installed the bypass relay in the DX-50, changed the audio input, and installed the BNC cable for external excitation.

We brought the DX up into the dummy load at 5 kW. We made sure that when the exciter was in the bypass mode, we were, in fact, operating on the internal oscillator and when not in bypass, we were operating on the external excitation from the exciter.

We then needed to set up the internal AM reference in the exciter. This is done by putting our Optimod 9200 into test-tone mode and watching the reference signal from the exciter on a scope. We set the exciter for 100 percent negative modulation, then fired up the DX, IBOC carriers off, and adjusted the gain on the interface box to produce a 100 percent modulated signal into the dummy. So far, so good.

Next, we turned on the IBOC carriers with the transmitter set for 5 kW. The display on the spectrum analyzer looked good, but on the receiver, the audio sounded awful in digital and analog. It was time to troubleshoot. Turns out the analog to digital (A/D) converter between the STL switcher and processing was bad. A quick replacement of the A/D resulted in clean audio.

There are several adjustments to make on the IBOC exciter. One major adjustment sets the phasing delay (from AM stereo, remember setting the group delay through the transmitter?) of the IBOC waveform as it passes through the transmitter. This is done by making an adjustment on the touch screen of the IBOC exciter while monitoring data errors on the receiver, or by watching the RF signal on a spectrum analyzer to minimize "spectral regrowth" around ± 20 kHz from carrier. I'm happy to say that errors on the WOR signal are zero and it is extremely stable.

The next adjustment was to adjust the delay of the analog signal to precisely match the delay of the digital signal. The reason for this adjustment and the delay added to the analog is that the radios are designed to lock on a station in analog mode, then, when the digital signal is acquired, blend or cross-fade into the digital signal. Obviously, if the two signals are not time aligned, the listener will hear an abrupt switch between them. Additionally, the radios are designed so that, if the digital signal is lost, the radio will immediately revert back to the analog signal. Once again, if the signals are not time aligned, the change will be abrupt.

The easiest way to do this? We set the receiver to produce the digital signal on the left, the analog on the right, and proceeded to match them by ear! The result is that there is no abrupt change when the receiver blends.

We then brought the DX up to 50 kW (all the above tests were done at a lower power level such that the dummy would not get grumpy and take up smoking). Analog sounded really good. Digital, being that the processing is very light (as opposed to our analog which is very "in-your-face"), sounded close to FM quality. Then … GLITCH. The DX-50 reduced its power to 25 kW, and ramped back up to 50 kW. We thought the problem might be that the dummy, which admittedly needs some work, was shifting impedance, so it was time to put the DX-50 back on the air.

ON-AIR TESTING: We switched back to the DX-50. It sounded really good in analog. We turned on the IBOC carriers. It sounded wonderful in digital. Then … GLITCH. The DX abruptly dropped to 25 kW, then ramped back up to 50 kW. It did this several times. Pat said he had seen this before.

A call to Harris showed that on the bandpass filter VSWR monitoring, the voltage and current sample points are taken in different locations along the circuit. At some point during operation, the zero crossing points of the voltage and current due to the phase modulation of the transmitter must occur at the same moment in time. The VSWR circuit takes this as a problem in the bandpass filter, and reduces the transmitter's power for protection.

As a band-aid, per Harris, we have bypassed the bandpass filter VSWR circuit. Harris is working on a field modification that we will need to perform on our DX-50 in the near future.

Total time spent? About three hours. And IBOC is on the air.

RESULTS: Of course, Kerry and I rushed to our cars to see what the outcome was on the air. My car has a stock Ford AM stereo radio. Kerry has a high-end radio with a $2 AM section. Before iBiquity arrived for installation, we had reset our Optimod 9200 from its National Radio Systems Committe (NRSC) settings to a 5-kHz brick wall roll-off. We based the 5 k setting on our NRSC processing settings, and added our own equalization (EQ) curve. Listening on our car radios, we could barely tell a difference in the processing changes on the AM stereo radio, and could hear no difference at all on the high-end radio. And, since we're not modulating above 5 kHz, we are now louder on these radios than we were.

Once IBOC was on, we listened for artifacts. On the supposed "wideband" AM stereo radio, I need to turn the volume up to ear-splitting levels before I can hear any noise under the audio. On Kerry's radio, you cannot hear any artifacts of IBOC whatsoever.

WOR's listeners are extremely loyal and are a vocal bunch. If they hear something wrong, they do not hesitate to speak up and make it known that "their" radio station has a problem and they want it fixed NOW. Our calls from listeners have consisted mostly of people wanting to know how they can hear our digital signal and where they can buy the radios.

We have had a few negative comments. One was from a gentleman who was restoring a 1930s vintage Atwater Kent radio, and wanted to let us know he heard hiss when he tuned across WOR on either side of us. The other negative comments have come from a group of AM stereo fanatics in

New Jersey. These people live for the day AM stereo makes a come back. They are not listening on typical AM radios. They have verbally personally attacked both Kerry and myself, the radio station, and iBiquity. Keep in mind that this group thinks that AM radio is a high fidelity medium. They also started a rumor that WOR was operating illegally. The NRSC mask allows emissions to $-25\,dBc$ from 10 to 20 kHz. IBOC operation puts the IBOC carriers from 5 to 15 kHz at $-30\,dBc$, perfectly legal.

The other complaint was from a person who was trying to get WLW. They live not all that far from our transmitter. Unfortunately, the IBOC carriers occupy space in the NRSC mask around 700, and they were not able to DX in the near field of the WOR antenna. But since WOR is legal, there is not much that can be done for this person.

The spectrum on the WOR signal was basically textbook perfect. The entire signal fits very nicely under the NRSC mask and is completely legal. And, even with all the detuning aspects of WOR's antenna, the IBOC carriers are symmetrical.

And IBOC was installed without rebuilding our studios or replacing our STLs. The time spent for installation was about three hours, and we did it in the afternoon with the auxiliary transmitter on the air. If your antenna system is in reasonable shape, and your transmitter is of fairly recent vintage (i.e., not a 1955 BC-5P), you should lose very little time and spend the minimum amount of money putting IBOC on your AM station.

For more information, I would recommend iBiquity's Web site at www. ibiquity.com. Or call your Harris representative. They can provide you with details from their IBOC road show, and can even guide you as to whether your IBOC installation will be as uneventful and easy as was ours.

A.8 Radio world guest commentary

I have written numerous guest commentaries in *Radio World Magazine* over the years. Many of them have to do with incorrect and false information being spread about HD Radio operation. Here is one where I have responded to a gentleman who has done just that.

I just finished reading the letters in the "Readers Forum" in the March 10th edition of Radio World, and the letter entitled "Slingin' Hash" from Jim Jenkins stands out as having erroneous information regarding IBOC. While the industry has been ramping up for IBOC deployment, there has not been very much information available regarding IBOC deployment, and I believe many of the statements made by Jenkins and others have been brought about because of ignorance on the subject, and not necessarily through any fault of their own. The information is simply not readily available. I wish to address the four primary concerns brought up by Jenkins.

1. IBOC will make all radios in the United States obsolete – When is this going to happen? There is no mandate to shut off the analog carriers, and your analog radio, AM or FM, works just fine with IBOC. This isn't HDTV we're talking about, where the analog carriers have a definite cut-off date set by the FCC. Your radio won't be obsolete the day your favorite station turns on an IBOC carrier. I listened to WOR on the analog radio in my car for 14 months before I had an IBOC-capable radio to listen to, and this analog radio was far from obsolete. Anyone who tells you that your analog radio will be obsolete has no clue what they are talking about and does not have the facts. Eventually, though, the present radios will become obsolete when and if a mandate to turn off the analog modulation comes about. I do not see this day coming any time in the near future. We are most likely 20 years out for this to happen.

2. The cost to small town radio – Yes, there are costs involved to convert to IBOC. Once again, there is, at this time, no mandate or timetable to do so. We're constantly reading in the trade publications, Radio World included, about the loss of listenership in Radio. Much of this has to do with the programming, which is beyond the scope of this commentary. But when you have listeners leaving for a service such as XM or Sirius, and they then discover that your station offers programming locally similar to what they like on these services, very frankly, your 1955 vintage transmitter won't cut it with them. Small town radio, much like small town television has had to do with HDTV, will need to eventually convert to IBOC, and the time to start planning and budgeting is now, not when and if the FCC mandates digital service. I would start planning to do this at some time down the road relatively soon and not ignore the fact that digital service is coming to AM and FM radio. If you put your head in the sand and pull it out to be confronted with a mandate to do it, you will be in trouble. Planning now will help soften the blow.

3. The listeners, particularly in poorer areas, won't be buying the new radios for years – And we should stop progress for the stations that are not in poor areas? How long did it take for FM and FM stereo to catch on? How long did it take for color television to catch on? It is going to be the same for IBOC implementation. It will take a while. No one has said that it will not. If we don't move forward, you may find that all stations, particularly those in poorer areas, will be in big

trouble in 10–15 years. Imagine radio listenership continuing on a downward spiral so that the poorer stations sign off first, as they will be the first to struggle and go belly up. Will IBOC be the savior of radio? No. But with digital services being in demand by consumers, it will help. We can't ignore this.

4. No one in the "trades" has addressed the adjacent-channel, sideband, frequency response curve and modulation limitation questions – I'm frequently a contributor in this particular trade. Ready for these issues to be addressed?

There are no modulation limitations. WOR is still banging away at -97 percent, $+122$ percent with the IBOC carriers on, with very aggressive processing, the same as we were pre-IBOC. This was a specification we put onto iBiquity when WOR became a test station in 2002. We do not lose analog loudness when the IBOC carriers come on at sunrise, and we do not gain analog loudness when the IBOC carriers go off at sunset.

We are still louder and prouder than our immediate competitors and make no apologies for that. IBOC did not hurt WOR's analog modulation. We have checked with oscilloscopes and spectrum analyzers.

We have discovered, however, a few radios that seem to have a broader bandwidth in the sampling for the automatic gain control (AGC) circuit than the frequency response the radio can reproduce. On these few radios, WOR's analog audio appears to reduce slightly when the AGC circuit senses the additional power in the sidebands when the IBOC carriers are turned on. These radios are few and far between and, very frankly, I see this as a design flaw with the radio. Here in the New York metropolitan area, there are a few AM stations that are awfully close together frequency-wise. I suspect these radios have the same issue with these close-spaced stations. Should we abandon IBOC because there are a few radios in the market with an inherently flawed design? Should we abandon the space program because there have been a few space shuttle accidents?

WOR has worked extremely closely with iBiquity's engineers to make sure that not only is the IBOC portion of the signal the best it can be, but that the analog portion of the signal is not impacted. I recall one software change where a mistake was made in the analog side of the software, the result being no real positive peak capability above $+100$ percent, and a distinct audio distortion. We identified the problems for iBiquity, and gave them one week to solve the issue before we would pull the IBOC carrier. They listened, resolved the issue, and then had a problem with the analog audio filtering. This resulted, two days later, in the "WOR Patch," which has since been incorporated into the final version of the software. We would not let the analog suffer, and iBiquity came through. The result is that there is no impact on analog performance, while the new HDC codec has solved the artifact issues with the PAC codec that we started with.

What needs to be addressed with the frequency response curve? On the analog carrier, you are limited to 5 kHz. In actuality, WOR is limiting to 6 kHz. The majority of AM radios I have encountered generally do not reproduce anything above 3–4 kHz. The stock radio that was in my Ford Explorer reproduced 6 kHz, but only when I was sitting in front of the transmitter building. So, what is the issue? Extending your analog frequency response beyond 6 kHz (again, discovered in WOR testing) will severely degrade your digital coverage area and digital performance. And we are running a modified NRSC equalization curve in the analog processing. Operating with a 6-kHz audio bandwidth proved to have a better sound even on typical narrow-band AM radios and did not affect the IBOC coverage of WOR, so we see no reason to limit our frequency response to 5 kHz. Since the greater portion of AM radios cannot "hear" anything above 4 kHz, I ask again, what is the issue?

Another little known fact is that there are two general operating modes for hybrid AM IBOC. The normal mode, which limits the analog frequency response to 5 kHz, allows the HD Radio to constantly look at the sidebands and decide which one to decode the data from, upper or lower. In testing with iBiquity, we discovered that there are distinct differences in how the sidebands will be recovered at any given receiving location dependent on many factors.

The second mode of IBOC operation allows for an analog bandwidth of 8 kHz. In this mode, however, the radio must decode both sidebands at all times to recover the data and generate HD audio. Obviously, if there is a problem with one of the sidebands, or if one of the sidebands is severely diminished (in the WOR null, far field, our upper sideband all but disappears), the radio cannot reproduce an HD signal. This will have the effect of reducing your HD coverage, and the recovered data will not be as robust. The choice of operation is up to the individual station, but if the majority of radios do not reproduce analog audio above about 4 kHz, what is the point of limiting your HD coverage?

ADJACENT CHANNEL AND SIDEBAND QUESTIONS – Yes, there may be some issues due to the IBOC sidebands. Once again, no one has ever said that there might not be. However, you first need to consider that the IBOC system is designed to fit under the NRSC mask as mandated by the FCC. Energy that fits under the mask is completely permissible under FCC regulations, regardless of what anyone wishes to read into this rule.

One should refer to the FCC regulations, Part 73.37, to get the definition of the coverage area for a particular class of AM station. Yes, contrary to what some people believe, there are coverage definitions in the FCC rules for AM stations. There may be some background hiss heard out around and beyond the 0.5-mV/m contour of a station that has an IBOC neighbor. In listening tests, this was deemed more acceptable than the "Donald Duck Talk" from present adjacent sideband splatter. And let's face it. In most areas of the country, if you can even hear an AM station out to the 0.5-mV/m contour because of the general electrically noisy environments we live in, you're a lucky dog. If you can't hear the station reliably in these areas anyway, there should be no reason to prevent implementation of IBOC.

If you think your typical listeners are listening to your station when the signal degrades to noise out to and beyond the 0.5-mV/m contour, perhaps you should do a study or survey of the average American's radio-listening habits. I observe my 16-year-old son, his friends, and my neighbors. My son knows what AM radio is (he'd better, considering what his old man does for a living!), yet he and his friends refuse to listen to AM radio. They simply do not care for the sound of it. And this has nothing to do with programming. One of his friends is a die-hard New York Yankees fan. The only time I heard him listening to a ball game on the radio was when the playoffs were carried by an FM station out of Newburgh, New York, near where we live. I have observed neighbors punching the button at the first sign of noise on an AM or an FM station. They don't like it, won't put up with it, and won't listen to a station regardless of the programming, once the signal gets noisy.

At this time, I won't get into the issue of the fact that we have essentially lost an entire generation of listeners to AM radio. But for those who believe that every listener is an avid DXer, I firmly believe you are kidding yourself. Stay the course and not change to accommodate the younger listeners who have grown up on Internet audio and MP3 players, and you will drive even more nails into the coffin of AM Radio and radio in general.

Jenkins states that we have a mindless push to a flawed technology. Show me any technology that is inherently perfect. There are none. Jenkins further states that we are going digital because it's "different." I have made countless recordings (on linear Digital Audio Tape (DAT)) off my IBOC car radio, and play them to WOR staff members (not just engineers), clients, and listeners who happen to be in the station ... on studio monitor speakers. I have given sales staff and neighbors CDs and asked them to listen to them in the car and tell me what they find objectional. Universally, all the people who have participated in these tests find it hard to believe that these recordings were made off of an AM radio (granted, IBOC capable), and ask when it will be available on more stations. They also ask where they can get one of these HD Radios. The AM HD sounds very good. I've been listening to it critically in the car since December. I can't imagine going back to the standard AM on my drive in the morning. The WOR Morning Show sounds so much better in the HD environment.

And while Jenkins makes the point that independent record companies like to press vinyl, walk into any music store or the music department in any K-Mart or Wal-Mart. Do a ratio of CDs to vinyl. What do you find? The CD has replaced vinyl as the universal recording and distribution medium. People download MP3 files all the time and find them more than acceptable to listen to. I don't buy the argument that because "old-fashioned records" give a warmer feel that they must be superior. Each medium has its pros and cons. Vinyl records are susceptible to surface noise, turntable rumble, typically have only 30-dB stereo separation, and generally have a maximum 50-dB signal-to-noise ratio. In this argument, the CDs have won.

Regarding the cascading of algorithms, yes, with IBOC, we're all going to have to be more careful regarding data reduction use. At WOR, we record the Bill O'Reilly program for later playback, and do so in what can be considered a worst case scenario. We pull the program down at our transmitter on Starguide MP2, send it to the studios on an MP3 channel on a T1, record it into our ENCO system MP2, play it back and send it to the transmitter via a linear digital channel on a T1, and then put it through the HDC codec. Listening in the car, you don't hear any "swimming" or raunchy data cascade effects. The average listener won't notice. If, however, you put the air product up against a studio recording of the O'Reilly program, you will definitely hear the result of the algorithm cascading.

Yes, we did this test with Westwood One, recording identical segments at every point in the path where the audio coding would change. Studio receives off the phone line from the Fox studios at the Westwood One head end here in Manhattan at the output of a Starguide receiver, at the output of our MP3 card on the T1, at the output of the ENCO playback, and off of an HD-capable radio. It's amazing to hear the changes along each leg of the path.

The overall result, however, is that no one will notice, unless he or she either knows what the studio product sounds like or is an audiophile listener. Don't forget – audio memory is extremely short. Unless you know what you are listening for, chances are you wont notice, unless the result of the cascading is so raunchy that you can't help but notice.

Now, before I am once again accused (and it was here in letters to Radio World) of being anti–small market radio and anti-AM in general, consider this. Buckley Broadcasting is one of the true small operators left in the United States. WOR is an anomaly in our company, as most of our stations are small stations in much smaller markets. We don't have the deep pockets of investors to pick as do the Clear Channels and Infinity's of the world. When we make a technology decision, it is something the company must believe in, and it is my job to bring the pros and cons of any new technology facing the company to the president. We are presently in the process of finding out what it is going to cost to outfit our 19 radio stations for IBOC operation. While this discovery, budgeting, and planning are taking place, I have discovered that iBiquity has reduced licensing rates at the date of this writing. While Buckley Broadcasting is not yet ready to implement IBOC operation on our other stations at this particular moment in time, I have recommended that the Corporation license all of our stations with iBiquity now at the reduced rates. It would have been irresponsible of me not to make this recommendation. I grew up on AM radio but I am a realist. If we continue on the "keep it the same because, after all, we're Radio!" path, we will all be in trouble.

IBOC isn't the three-headed monster, the fear mongers among us think it is. It's time for a change in our industry. Education is the key to understanding and using this new technology to our greatest advantage. Remaining the same while the world marches past us will definitely place terrestrial AM and FM broadcasting among the dinosaurs and make us irrelevant.

A.9 Conclusions

I thank you for the purchase of this book. I hope that it has helped you gain the knowledge you need to add HD Radio operation to your station. I also hope that my observations in this appendix have helped you through my experiences with HD Radio.

As I stated in the opening section, broadcasting as we know it is in a constant change of flux. This is certainly an exciting time to be in the business. The digital future is at hand – and it is in your and my hands. While you may not fully agree with HD Radio, I hope you agree that it is our job to make it work the best it can. I hope you have a very successful HD Radio install!

Bibliography

Salek S. (2007) NRSC analog and digital radio standards, in: Williams E., Jones G., Layer D., Osenkowsky T. (Eds.), NAB Engineering Handbook, 10th ed., National Association of Broadcasters/Focal Press, Washington, DC, pp. 111-115.

Mendenhall G.N. (2007) FM and digital radio transmitters, in: Williams E., Jones G., Layer D., Osenkowsky T. (Eds.), NAB Engineering Handbook, 10th ed., National Association of Broadcasters/Focal Press, Washington, DC, pp. 777-823.

Surette R.A. (2007) FM combining systems, in: Williams E., Jones G., Layer D., Osenkowsky T. (Eds.), NAB Engineering Handbook, 10th ed., National Association of Broadcasters/Focal Press, Washington, DC, pp. 875-895.

Detweiler J. (2007) AM and FM IBOC equipment and systems, in: Williams E., Jones G., Layer D., Osenkowsky T. (Eds.), NAB Engineering Handbook, 10th ed., National Association of Broadcasters/Focal Press, Washington, DC, pp. 921-968.

Maxson D.P. (2007) The IBOC Handbook: Understanding HD Radio Technology, National Association of Broadcasters/Focal Press, Washington, DC.

Index

Edwards Brothers Inc.
Ann Arbor MI. USA
March 22, 2012